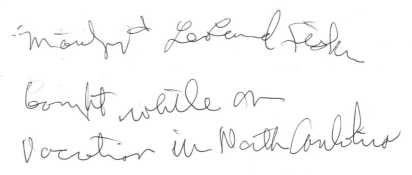

# SOUTHWESTERN INDIAN CEREMONIALS

## by Tom Bahti and Mark Bahti

**_Tom Bahti_** The late Tom Bahti, a graduate in anthropology from the University of New Mexico, was a well-regarded dealer in Indian art who was nationally recognized as an authority on the arts, crafts, and culture of Southwestern Indians. He was deeply involved in the future of the people of the Southwest.

**_Mark Bahti_** Mark Bahti, like his father, has authored a number of books on the arts and culture of the tribes of the Southwest. He is also active in several Indian-run organizations that seek to provide educational and economic development opportunities for members of the Indian community.

## INDEX

# Introduction

Religion has been described as man's attempt to control those forces which lie beyond the glow of his campfire, and it matters little whether the reference is made to a small band of hunters huddled in a cave around a cooking fire or a modern city dweller who cringes before the prospect of a nuclear fireball destroying his modern metropolis. The basic need is identical.

When discussing religion, either one's own or someone else's, it is best not to be too concerned with logic, for all mythology, whether based on written or spoken traditions, is singularly illogical. A Christian, for example, may find no inconsistency in acceptance of the Commandment "thou shalt not kill," along with acceptance of capital punishment, armies (with the chaplains that serve them), biological and chemical warfare along with nuclear weapons, but rationalization for this is based not on logic but on an unquestioning belief in the myths of his own society. In examining the religion of another society, however, he may not be as tolerant or understanding and instead be either indignant or condescendingly amused if all beliefs cannot be neatly and logically pigeonholed into an instantly comprehensive concept.

*Further complications arise with the tremendous variation in understanding and degree of belief among members of any religious sect. The range of belief extends from fanatically devout to passively indifferent in all groups. It is less accurate to say, "All Christians believe that..." than to say, "Most (or some) Christians believe that..."*

*Attempts to translate religious concepts from one language to another cause additional confusion; there is no equivalent in the English language vocabulary, for example, for the Zuni word* kokko, *or the Hopi word* katsina. *Conversely, the Zunis have no equivalent for the English word* religion; *they regard religion as being inseparable from life itself.*

*The brief descriptions that follow are not intended to represent Southwestern Indian ceremonials as "peculiar" or "quaintly colorful," but simply as attempts by fellow human beings to meet a basic need in ways that are merely different from our own.*

*Superstition, it should be recalled, is the* other *man's religion.*

— Tom Bahti, 1970.

# Native Religions and Foreign Influences

That native ceremonies are still held by the Indians of the Southwest is a tribute to their way of life and the strength of their religious beliefs.

From prehistoric times to the present it has been customary for the various tribes in the Southwest to borrow from each other's religion. If one group performed a particularly effective ceremony, it could be learned from them and performed as one's own. Dances, songs, and rituals were freely adopted and adapted, and the practice continues today.

It was not uncommon even for traditional enemies to borrow each other's ceremonials. Much of Navajo mythology, for example, was adapted from Pueblo tribes, and the Hopi possess a number of katsinas they recognize as being of Navajo origin. The similarities in the emergence myths of many Southwestern tribes indicate a sharing of legends as well.

No group presumed its religion to be superior to that of another, and certainly no tribe ever conducted warfare against another for the purpose of forcing its religious beliefs upon them. It must have been bewildering, therefore, to find that the European invaders of the Southwest made a special effort to stamp out native beliefs in order to impose their own religious doctrines.

## THE SPANIARDS

The Spaniards explored, conquered, and settled the Southwest to harvest gold for the Crown and souls for the Church. Civil and Church authorities regarded the native people as barbarians, completely devoid of civilization and Christianity. It was not a matter of replacing one culture with another since they did not believe the Indians *had* a culture.

In the name of "civilizing" and "Christianizing" the Indians, katsina masks along with any and all other religious objects were destroyed.

Many Indian groups incorporate aspects of Christianity into their traditional religions. While this practice may frustrate missionaries, the Pueblo Indians prefer to practice religious tolerance.

"Idolaters" were confined in stocks, and flogging was commonly used to enforce the Spanish prohibition against Indian religious observances. But instead of stamping out native religions, the Spaniards merely drove them underground. Several minor rebellions and the Great Pueblo Revolt of 1680 are directly traceable to the harsh punishment meted out to religious leaders.

The Church finally learned to live side by side with native religion, though it is doubtful whether it was—or is—as tolerant of Indian religions as the Indian is of Western religions.

The American invasion of the Southwest, which followed the 1848 Treaty of Guadalupe Hidalgo, had no immediate effect on native religions. Catholic missions continued to operate and the Pueblo Indians made nominal use of them while adhering to native beliefs.

In the 1870s and '80s, the U.S. government adopted a policy of turning over the task of "civilizing" Indians to the churches, and various Christian denominations were assigned to specific reservations. The practice was discontinued in the 1890s, but not before the influence of some 27 Christian sects became established among a number of tribes, particularly those whose native culture had been reduced to a state of disintegration.

*Preceding pages: Looking east to the Hopi villages of Second Mesa and Corn Rock. Photo by Owen Seumptewa.*

When European missionaries first arrived in the New World they attempted to suppress all forms of "heathen idolatry," refusing to recognize them as religions. Missions were established in most of the pueblos, and many still stand today. After the Great Pueblo Revolt of 1680, the Church developed a degree of tolerance toward Indian religious practices. It was not until 1934 that the U.S. government extended the concept of religious freedom to Indian religions.

MARK BAHTI

## GOVERNMENT SUPPRESSION OF NATIVE RELIGION

About this same time, the Bureau of Indian Affairs, which was originally under the War Department, made a number of attempts to suppress native religions with a series of departmental regulations. It is ironic that the very people who took inordinate pride in the fact that their immigrant ancestors came to this country to escape religious persecution tolerated such a move. Begun as a frightened reaction to the Ghost Dance movement of the 1880s, which claimed to foretell the disappearance of the white man as well as the return of the buffalo and the old ways, the regulations were also directed against the Sun Dance of the Plains tribes and the rising strength of the Native American Church.

This anti-Indian movement culminated in 1889 with a set of regulations known as the Code of Religious Offenses. It was used as late as the 1920s in an attempt to crush Pueblo religion, restricting the time of year and days of the week for native religious observances. It even restricted the number of participants and set age limits—all in an attempt to deny younger Indians the opportunity to participate and learn.

In a specific campaign against Taos, the religious leaders were accused of being "half-animal" in their practice of "sadistic" and "obscene" pagan religion. And if that was not enough to swing public opinion against them, one U.S. senator declared them and their Anglo supporters to be un-American and agents of Moscow.

It was not until 1934 that this policy was reversed. Under John Collier's administration as Commissioner of Indian Affairs, the following directive was issued: "No interference with Indian religious life or ceremonial expression will hereafter be tolerated. The cultural liberty of Indians is in all respects to be considered equal to that of any non-Indian group." Freedom of religion, the goal of so many early white immigrants, was thereby finally extended to America's original inhabitants.

The impact of Christianity upon Southwestern Indian religions is difficult to summarize except in broad generalizations. A minority accepted the new religion to the complete abandonment of native practices. A majority merely accommodated the new doctrines by modifying them to fit with native beliefs (much as the tribes borrowed from each other's religions)—this was primarily the case with the Rio Grande pueblos. The Yaquis modified Catholicism into a form that was not recognized by the Roman Catholic Church, but which suited their needs. Others, such as the followers of the Native American Church (Peyote Cult) combined native and Christian beliefs to form an entirely new religious movement. And, of course, a surprising number, notably among the Hopi and Zuni, practice their native religions to the total exclusion of Christian beliefs.

# Navajo

### THE EMERGENCE MYTH

In the beginning, First Man and First Woman were transformed from an ear of corn. It was they who led the people during the Emergence.

The world today, by Navajo reckoning, is the fifth to be inhabited by the First People. (Other estimates vary from 4 to 16.) The four previous worlds were located underground, each one a different color, but none of them contained light. The First People lived in each of these worlds successively until they finally ascended to this world by making their way through a hollow reed. The "Place of Emergence" or "Center-of-the-Universe" is believed to be a badger hole in the mountains of southeastern Colorado.

At first the land was covered with water, a wet and disagreeable place, but in time the Holy People (another name for the First People) transformed the earth into a livable place, and defined the boundaries of Navajoland. Mount Taylor, in New Mexico, is the Southern or Turquoise Mountain; Mount Humphrey, in the San Francisco Peaks near Flagstaff, is the Western or Abalone Mountain. There is a difference of opinion over the exact identification of the Northern (Jet) and Eastern (White Shell) mountains. Light was created by First Man and First Woman who fashioned the moon, sun, and stars of precious stones. An orderly arrangement of the stars was upset when the ever-present trickster, Coyote, scattered them about the sky.

Evil existed in the form of monsters who had also come up from the underworlds and now began to kill many of the Earth People. At this time, a cradleboard containing a baby girl clothed in light magically appeared. She grew to become Changing Woman, sometimes identified as Earth with its constantly changing seasons, or as Nature itself. Changing Woman eventually married Sun and Water and gave birth to twin boys, Monster Slayer and Born-of-Water. (In some versions of the story Changing Woman— or Turquoise Woman—and her sister White Shell

Navajo sandpainting ceremonies are part of a healing ritual that includes songs, chants, prayers, and herbs. Recognizing the important role of the patient's frame of mind in the healing process, hospitals and clinics on the reservation often work with Navajo hatathli—medicine men—in the treatment of patients.
Andy Tsinajinnie

Navajo oral tradition includes stor... legends, and religious practices ... are interrelated, intricately detailed, a... highly complex. According to Nav... belief, they must be preserved d... to the smallest detail. To properly le... the oral traditions requires car... listening and begins in childho... Harrison Be...

*To become a* hatathli *requires years of careful study and practice as an apprentice. This young Navajo sheepherder is beginning his lifelong study of the Navajo traditions and stories that are crucial to the success of a good medicine man. Harrison Begay*

Woman married, respectively, Sun and Water and gave birth to the Twin War Gods.)

The exploits of the Twin War Gods form a goodly part of Navajo mythology. In their journeys they encountered, and succeeded in slaying, many of the monsters that were bothering the Earth People. They failed only in dispatching Old Age, Poverty, Sickness, and Death. Throughout Navajo country is evidence of the Twins' battles. A lava flow east of Grants, New Mexico, is the dried blood of a slain monster. Shiprock is the remains of a man-eating eagle, and various volcanic peaks are the heads of monsters decapitated by the Twins.

It was Changing Woman who finally created human beings, using flakes of skin from her own body. She formed six groups of people, believed by some to represent the first Navajo clans. There is no supreme being in Navajo religion. The most powerful and most important deities include Changing Woman, Sun, and the Twin War Gods. Of these only Changing Woman is consistently helpful to people. Changing Woman lives on an island in the Western Sea where she is visited daily by her husband, the Sun. All other deities are capable of helping or harming, and are sometimes classified on the basis of how difficult they are to persuade to be helpful.

Lesser deities include *ye'iis*—the male and female figures that are depicted in sandpaintings and represent forces found in nature such as wind, thunder, and lightning. Below them on the list of Holy People are the ancestors of animals and plants, and figures identified with specific geographical locations.

## AFTERWORLD

The Anglo concept of an Indian's "Happy Hunting Ground" does not apply to the Navajo—nor to many Indian tribes, for that matter. *This* is the life that is important. It is not considered as mere preparation for another world. Neither is there a concept of another world for eternal punishment. The Afterworld is a shadowy and ill-defined, dull but not unpleasant place, an underground "to the north" which is reached by four days' travel after death.

Death is considered inevitable and therefore not so much feared as the dead themselves. Since the deceased are always a possible source of *chindi*, or malevolent ghosts, they are disposed of as quickly as possible and with strict performance of all required rituals. Any error may offend the deceased and cause the chindi to seek revenge.

*The Twin War Gods, Born-of-Water and Monster Slayer, were given weapons by their father, the Sun, that enabled them to slay most of the monsters who plagued humankind. (A few, like poverty, sickness, and lice, managed to survive.) Here one of the Twins attacks the Monster Bird who used to attack and eat unwary travelers. His petrified remains are known in English as Shiprock, in northwestern New Mexico. Navajoland is dotted with evidence of the Twins' great battles. Andy Tsinajinnie*

*In Navajo culture, as with most Indian cultures in the Southwest, corn pollen is gathered for religious purposes. A symbol of the promise of fertility and the renewal of the cycle of life, corn pollen is a vital part of any prayer or prayer offering. The Navajo believe that if a prayer is offered correctly, with a good heart, it will be answered. For some the yellow pollen also symbolizes the yellow light of the life-giving morning sun. A. C. Begay*

*Most Navajo healing songs are accompanied by a rattle.*

*The sandpaintings or* ikaah *used in Navajo healing rites are made of ground rocks and plant matter—all collected within the traditional boundaries of Navajoland. These images are begun after sunrise and must be completed by sunset. Their remains are then taken a safe distance away for a ceremonial burial.*

## CURING CEREMONIES

The Navajo concept of the Universe in an ideal state is one in which all parts—each with its power for good and evil—are maintained in inter-related harmony—*hozho.* The balance, at best, is precarious and may be upset intentionally by ghosts or witches, or unintentionally by persons who break a religious taboo or unwittingly come in contact with snakes, bears, or lightning. To cross the path of a bear or touch a piece of wood that came from a lightning-struck tree is enough to upset the balance.

Illness, whether physical or mental, results from upsetting the harmony. Conversely, the cure for illness is to restore the patient to harmony. It is to this end—the preservation or restoration of harmony or *hozho*—that Navajo religious ceremonies are performed.

To determine the cause of a particular illness is the job of a diagnostician—*ndilniihii* or "hand trembler." Prayer, concentration, and the application of sacred pollen to the patient causes the priest-practitioner's hand to tremble—it is from these movements that the exact cause of the illness is determined.

The cause of the sickness determines the ceremony or "sing" needed to effect a cure. Also called "chants" or "ways," these sings are based on Navajo mythology. They consist of complicated ceremonies lasting from one to nine nights, and can include the use of chants, songs, prayers, dances, prayer sticks, herbs, emetics, sweat baths, and sandpaintings, all performed under the direction of a "singer," or priest-practitioner, known in Navajo as a *hatathli.*

There are six main groups of chants or song ceremonials, although some have become obsolete through disuse. The Blessingway rites are not curing rites, but are performed for general well-being, to ensure, as the Navajos put it, that one may "walk in beauty."

The curing ceremonials or chantways are concerned with specific illnesses. The Bead Chant cures skin disease. The Shooting Chant is used against disease attributable to lightning or snakes. Insanity and paralysis usually require the Night Chant, while nervousness can be alleviated with the Mountainway. The Windway cures disease caused by evil winds and covers a host of afflictions ranging from poor vision, insomnia, and hoarseness to tuberculosis, heart trouble, snakebite, and even alcoholism.

There are probably over 50 chants or ways, not counting the variations. Most singers or priest-practitioners know no more than two or three complete chants and specialize in those. It would be impossible for one man to know all of the complicated rituals for over a dozen curing rites. If a chant is not performed precisely it will not cure, and instead can cause harm to befall those present.

The performance of a lengthy curing rite is an expensive affair, and taxes the finances of the patient's entire extended family. Not only is the hatathli well paid, but tremendous quantities of

*The Navajo Ye'ii Bichaii Dance is part of a nine-day*
*healing ceremony known as the Night Chant.*
*A Navajo medicine man carrying a*
*basket of sacred cornmeal for blessings, walks*
*ahead of a ye'ii known as Talking God,*
*who is in turn followed by seven other ye'ii.*
*Johnny Secatero*

food must be provided for guests—and they arrive from far and wide to share the blessings derived from attending the ceremonies, and to take part in the related social activities.

The patient, through the rituals, becomes purified and eventually identified with the deity whose help is sought. From them he obtains power and overcomes the evil causing the illness, thereby restoring him to harmony with the Universe. Once again he "walks in beauty." The sense of security and well-being the patient derives from the host of friends, family, and fellow tribespeople who surround him during the ceremony is also conducive to his recovery.

*This Ye'ii Bichaii dancer is known in Navajo as*
B'ganaskiddy. *The name does not translate and*
*consequently some bizarre names, like Camel God,*
*have been given to this being who carries the seeds of*
*living plants in his pack. Sometimes referred to as*
*Harvest God, he is far more complex than such a*
*simple name suggests. Bruce Watchman*

*Nahas'tsan Beh'assun* and *Yaa-diklith Beh'hasteen* *are known in English as Mother Earth and Father Sky. In the center of Mother Earth are the four sacred plants—corn, beans, squash, and tobacco. (The latter is sometimes used in praying or purifying.) The night sky is symbolized in Father Sky, including the Milky Way (the zigzag lines across his shoulders) with key constellations and stars.*

### SANDPAINTINGS

Sandpaintings, probably the best-known portion of the lengthy, complex Navajo curing ceremonies, are used in various religious rites by most tribes in the Southwest. The Navajos, however, have developed them to the greatest degree and recognize between 600 and 1,000 separate designs.

Dry paintings, as they are sometimes called, use pulverized minerals to form the patterns although vegetal material such as pollen and cornmeal may also be used. They range in size from 1 to 20 feet across, and may require a dozen or more persons working most of a day to complete. The sandpainting is created, used, and destroyed between sunrise and sunset of a single day.

The sandpainting is a symbolic representation of some portion of Navajo mythology. The patient is seated on the sandpainting after it is completed, and parts of it are placed on the patient's body. By identifying in this way with the deities invoked, power is gained from them. The evil that has caused the sickness is absorbed by the sand and is then ceremonially buried.

The colors used in Navajo dry paintings are usually symbolic of direction. As a general rule white is east, blue (a female color) is south, yellow is west, and black (male) is north, while red represents sunshine.

The Night Chant or Nightway—more commonly referred to as the *Ye'ii Bichaii*—is a major winter curing ceremony that can be held only after the snakes are asleep and there is no longer danger of lightning. The rite can be performed to cure patients of nervousness or insanity. It is a dangerous ritual, for mistakes made by either the patient or singer during its performance can cause crippling, facial paralysis, loss of sight, or loss of hearing.

The name Ye'ii Bichaii is used for the Nightway because of the appearance of numerous *ye'iis* (supernatural beings that possess great powers) during the last two nights of this nine-day annual ceremony.

On the eighth day the ye'ii bichaiis conduct an initiation rite to introduce Navajo children to the secret of the masked gods. The children first have their hair washed—a standard act of purification among most Southwestern tribes—and then white clay is daubed on their bodies.

The boys are blessed with sacred meal and then ceremonially whipped with yucca leaves by the masked figures. The girls are marked on the feet, hands, shoulders, and head with cornmeal and touched with ears of white and yellow corn wrapped in spruce twigs.

Shortly afterwards the ye'ii bichaiis remove their masks so that the children learn they are really ordinary human beings who only play the part of supernatural figures. *Hastseyalti*, the Talking God of the East, places his mask on each of the boys while the female *Hastse-baad* places hers on the girls so that each child may view the world through the eyes of the ye'ii bichaiis.

Adults often take part in this ritual for it is necessary for each Navajo to participate in the initiation ceremony four times during his lifetime.

Throughout the ninth night Ye'ii Bichaii dance teams perform, each group singing in the falsetto voice for which these dancers are noted.

*Unlike the katsinas of the Hopi, Navajo ye'ii bichaii are rarely carved. The very first set was probably made in the 1930s. There are, however, some similarities, ranging from the initiation of children into the secret of the masked dancers to the communal ownership of such masks, which forbids their ever being sold or otherwise removed from the tribe.*

*A central theme to well-being among the Navajo is the concept of* hozhon. *There is no one-word equivalent in English. Symbolized here by the rainbow guardian, it has to do with balance, harmony, and the beauty that arises from them.*
*James Wayne Yazzie*

## SQUAW DANCE

The *Entah* or Enemyway—mistakenly referred to as a Squaw Dance by non-Navajos—is a war ceremonial conducted only during the summer months. Formerly it was given as a purification rite for warriors who had been contaminated by contact with the enemy. Now it may be performed for persons whose sickness has been diagnosed as resulting from contact with whites or other non-Navajos.

The Entah is a three-day ritual that begins at the patient's hogan and moves to a new location on each succeeding day—usually a day's ride away by horseback. Much of the time between specific parts of the rite is spent in racing, gambling, and listening to informal talks by recognized leaders.

On the third day the Black Dancers—the clowns of the War Ceremony—perform a Mud ceremonial. Emerging from the smoke hole of a hogan, they seize the patient and toss him into the air. Afterwards they stretch him face down in a mudhole while they attempt to loosen the hold of the evil that is causing the sickness by running over the patient. After this ritual is completed, spectators are fair game and those caught are also given a mud bath.

The Round Dance is performed on the third night and is primarily a "coming out" event for eligible young females. The girls, with much encouragement from their mothers, invite young men to join them in a round dance. At the end of several rounds the man is required to make a token payment to the girl for the privilege of dancing with her. The Round Dance is an all-night affair performed to the accompaniment of a chorus and drummer.

## FIRE DANCE

The Mountain Chant or Mountainway is a winter ceremonial, to be given when there is the possibility that summer thunderstorms or spring windstorms might cause death by snakebite or lightning. The Mountain Chant gets its name from the dwelling place of the deities whose aid is invoked during the ceremony. The names Fire Dance or Corral Dance are derived from rituals performed as part of the nine-day ceremonial.

On the ninth day of the chant, a huge semicircular corral of evergreen is erected. It is here that medicine men perform magical feats: a yucca plant appears to grow and blossom in a matter of minutes; men swallow arrows; a feather dances unaided; or a sun symbol may climb out of a basket and up a pole and then return to its container.

Afterwards the Fire Dancers appear, daubed with white clay, and carrying torches of cedar bark that they light at the huge central fire. They dash in and out of the fire with impunity, lashing themselves and their fellow dancers with flaming torches. This is a purification ritual that completes the Mountain Chant. After the Fire Dance, spectators pick up bits of the charred cedar bark as a charm against fire.

*The Fire Dance occurs on the ninth night of the Mountainway. After the hatathli present perform certain magical feats, men daubed in white clay appear within an enclosure made of evergreen. Brandishing cedar bark torches, they dash in and out of a bonfire without harm. After this purification ritual, spectators gather bits of the charred bark as a charm against fire. Andy Tsinajinnie*

# Rio Grande Pueblos

### KERESAN EMERGENCE MYTH

The emergence myth varies somewhat in detail among the seven Keresan-speaking pueblos. The version given here relies primarily on accounts from Santa Ana and Santo Domingo pueblos.

In the beginning the people lived in the innermost of the Underworlds. Seeking light, they moved progressively upward through four worlds, each of a different color—white, red, blue, and yellow.

With the aid of various plants, animals, and birds an attempt was made to break through the crust of the present world. Finally a badger, standing on an eagle's nest built on top of a spruce tree, succeeded in enlarging a hole, made by a woodpecker, until it was big enough to allow people to pass through.

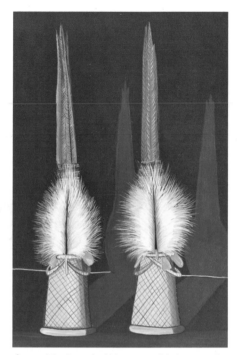

Corn Mother fetishes—which vary in appearance among tribes—are the most important fetish in most pueblo traditions. Roger Tsabetsaye

Assisted by *Iatiko*, Mother of All, they emerged at the *Sipapu*, the Place of Emergence or Center of the World. The world was wet and soft until the Sun, father of the Twin War Gods, dried it and made it habitable.

Sipapu was too sacred a place in which to dwell, so the people left to seek another location. Only Iatiko remained, but before the people left she gave them her heart—corn—and instructed the religious leaders to care for the people as she had done. She also told the people to return to Sipapu at death.

The people wandered about and finally settled at White House (an unidentified site "to the north" of their present villages). Here they dwelt with the deities who taught them all that was necessary for their life in this world. The katsinas appeared among them to dance for rain and the *Koshare* and *Kurena* came to help make the crops grow.

Although life was good at White House, eventually groups began to leave to seek new places—each became a new tribe in doing so. The Keresans also left and moved southward until

*The Deer Dance of the Tewa pueblos reflects the belief that a hunter will be unsuccessful if he does not first gain the deer's cooperation through showing respect. After a deer is killed, further rituals ensure that the deer's spirit will be reborn as another deer. Animals disappear only when hunted disrespectfully.*

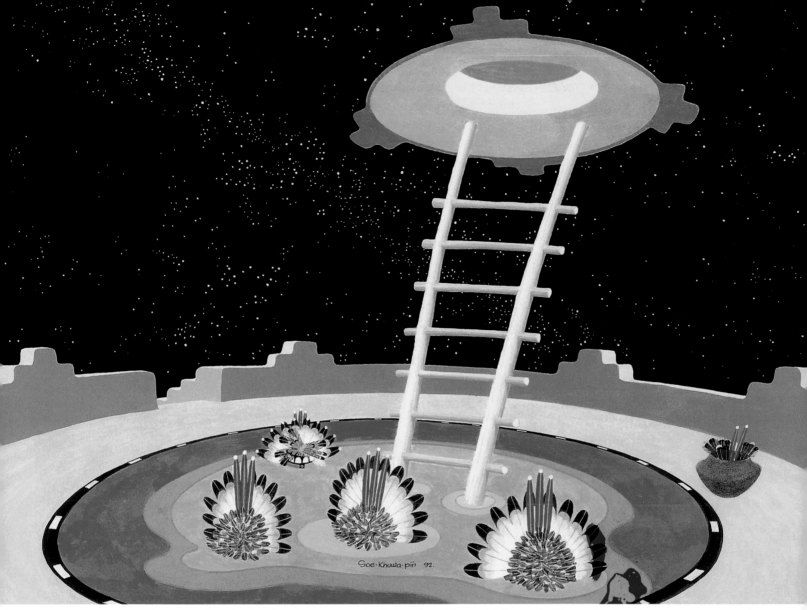

*The Emergence stories of many tribes in the Southwest speak of entering this world through either a body of water or through an opening in the sky. Many tribes tell of occupying a succession of previous worlds before arriving in this one. Taos legend states that they emerged at Blue Lake. Soe Khuwa-pin*

they reached their present locations. No longer do the masked gods live among the people, making it necessary now for the people themselves to impersonate the deities and perform the dances to ensure the well-being of the pueblos.

### THE CREATION AND COSMOS

Thought Woman, the deity who created all things by thinking them into existence, is responsible for the world as it appears. She may also be the same figure as Spider Grandmother, another deity to whom the same role is attributed.

The Keresans envisage the earth as the center of the universe with all other planets functioning in order to make the earth livable. The sun is referred to as "Father" and is an important deity. The sky is "in charge" of the earth and its people, and the earth is referred to as "Mother." Corn is also called "Mother."

### AFTERWORLD

At birth each person receives a soul and a guardian spirit from the Mother of All. At the time of death both the soul and the guardian leave the body but remain in the house of the deceased for four days before making the journey to Sipapu, the entrance to the Underworld. The guardian spirit carries a prayer stick, necessary for the admission of the soul to Sipapu. Depending on the virtue of the individual, the soul is assigned to one of the four Underworlds. Those qualified to enter the innermost world become *Shiwana* (Rainmakers) and return to the villages in the form of clouds.

Death is explained as a natural and necessary phenomenon for "if nobody died there would soon be no room left in the world."

Corn has always been the basis of Pueblo life. To maintain the precarious balance of an agricultural economy in this land of little rain requires the cooperation of all forces, natural and supernatural. It is not surprising, therefore, that all religious ceremonies (except for curing rites) revolve around the cultivation and propagation of corn.

Constant references to Earth Mother and Corn Mother indicate that agriculture is more than just a practical art; it goes far beyond to encompass the philosophy and religion of the Pueblo Indians.

The Corn Dance, commonly performed during the spring and summer months, may be given at any time. Although its purpose is always the propagation of corn, it may be performed to mark the annual installation of new secular officers of the pueblo, or the village's Catholic saint's day.

The dance, as with all Southwestern religious ceremonies, is a combination of song, drama, dance, and poetry which forms a prayer for rain, bountiful harvests, the propagation of animals and plants, and the well-being of the pueblo and all those who attend the ceremony.

All Rio Grande pueblos perform the Corn Dance. Perhaps the largest and most impressive is given at the village of Santo Domingo on the fourth of August—Saint Dominic's Day—the saint assigned to the village by the Catholic priests who accompanied the Spanish explorers.

Early in the morning of the fourth, Indians attend Mass at the church just outside the pueblo. On this day, baptisms and marriages are performed and recorded for the previous year. The statue of Saint Dominic is removed from the church, paraded through the village streets to

*Feast Day at Santa Clara is held on the Saint's day for Saint Claire, but the ceremonies observed pre-date Catholicism at this pueblo.*

the beating of a snare drum and the firing of guns, and then deposited in a temporary shelter of cottonwood branches in the dance plaza. The saint is guarded by the pueblo's officers, and the noise of guns and the snare drum continues while the dancers pay homage to Saint Dominic. After this, the day is devoted to the native ceremonial. Catholicism and Pueblo religion exist side by side, but there is no real mixing of the two.

The pueblo's population is divided into two moieties: the Squash or Winter People and the Turquoise or Summer People. (Each half is responsible for the village affairs during six months of the year.) The dancers of each moiety alternate performances during the day.

*Because of the centuries-long importance of corn to pueblo life, the Corn Dance is a ritual that is shared—though in varying forms—by all pueblos. This is a Tewa Corn Dance. Tonita Peña*

*Corn must be cultivated; if left to reseed by itself, the crop quickly dies out. This special relationship between the farmer and the plant has led it to be personified as both Corn Mother and Corn Maiden. Stories remind people of the respect that must be shown in tending the crop lest the corn maidens leave and famine follow. The Blue Corn Maiden represents one of the many color varieties of pueblo corn. Gilbert Atencio*

Each kiva, the Squash and the Turquoise, provides its own *Koshares*, chorus, drummer, standard bearer, and corn dancers—usually numbering over 200 persons. The bodies of the male Squash moiety dancers are painted with a yellow ochre, and those of the Turquoise are painted with a blue-gray clay.

The first figures to appear are the Koshares of the Turquoise moiety, with their bodies painted horizontally in black and white stripes and dressed in ragged black breechcloths. On their wrists and moccasins are worn strips of rabbit fur, and their hair is tied up in "horns" decorated with cornhusks. The *Kurena* of the Squash kiva are similarly attired except their bodies are divided vertically, with one half painted white with black spots and the other half yellow. Both wear deer-hoof rattles at the waist.

*The dancers during a ceremony, such as this feast day at San Ildefonso Pueblo, are accompanied by a chorus of men with drums. Their deep voices and drumming fill the plaza with sound.*

As invisible spirits of the deceased, the Koshare and Kurena possess much power to bring rain clouds and to influence the growth of crops. Related to the sun, their home is in the east. During the dance they magically protect the pueblo and its inhabitants from all enemies. They also perform many practical services for the dancers by making needed adjustments or repairs to the dancers' costumes during the ceremony.

As clowns they pantomime, with exaggerated gestures, the chorus or the dancers themselves. Between dances they indulge in ribald horseplay, much to the delight of the spectators and the chagrin of their victims.

The chorus, made up of 50 or more men and a drummer, are next to appear. They are dressed in loose-fitting, bright-colored shirts and trousers split at the ankle. Each carries sprigs of the evergreen—as a symbol of growing things and everlasting life. Although the chants follow a traditional rhythmic form, they are usually composed anew each year. The expressive movements of the chorus mimic the words that describe the gathering of the clouds from the four directions, the falling rain, and the growing plants.

The main procession of corn dancers is led by a man who bears the sun symbol. This consists of

*Known by different names among the different pueblo tribes, the Koshare is a clown who performs in ways that are both humorous and sacred. Koshares live in the east, home of the sun, and are able to bring rain clouds and influence the growth of crops. Geraldine Gutierrez*

a long pole (representing the fir tree that enabled the people to climb up from the Underworld) from which is suspended a dance kilt with eagle feathers and a fox pelt. Fastened to the end of the pole is a painted gourd (containing sacred seeds) and a dazzling cluster of macaw feathers. Under this banner the dancers perform. The waving of the sun symbol over the corn dancers constitutes both a blessing and a purification, and a request to the *Shiwana*—the Rainmakers or Rain Cloud People—to bless the pueblo with moisture.

The male corn dancers are dressed in white cotton kilts (this was formerly the ordinary attire of Pueblo men) embroidered with symbols of clouds and rain. Over this is tied the white, tasseled rain sash. From the back of the belt is suspended a fox skin, which some say is a reminder of man's common ancestry with animals, of a time when all had tails. Behind the right knee is tied a turtle-shell rattle with deer-hoof tinklers. In the right hand is a gourd rattle with which the sound of falling rain is imitated. Skunk fur worn over the moccasins protects the wearer from evil. A bandolier hung over the left shoulder is decorated with conus shells from the Pacific Ocean. A cluster of parrot feathers is worn on the top of the head—the plumage of this bird is believed to bring rain from the south. Personal jewelry and sprigs of evergreen complete their clothing.

The female dancers wear a black *manta*—blanket dress—tied at the waist with a red and green woven belt. In most pueblos the women dance barefoot. In each hand they carry evergreen boughs. Their hair hangs loose in imitation of the long wisps of summer rain that sweep the land. On their heads are worn *tablitas,* thin wooden boards cut in a terraced cloud pattern and either pierced or painted with sun, moon, or star designs.

*The Corn Dancer carries in her hands prayer offerings of turkey feathers and evergreens from the mountains. Her white sash with its long fringe is called a rain sash. On her* manta *(dress) are the inverted triangles that symbolize rain clouds, and in her hair macaw tail feathers are symbolic of the south, where summer rains originate.*
*Geraldine Gutierrez*

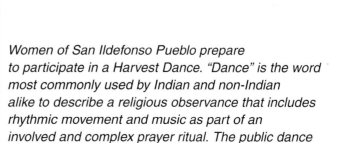

*Women of San Ildefonso Pueblo prepare to participate in a Harvest Dance. "Dance" is the word most commonly used by Indian and non-Indian alike to describe a religious observance that includes rhythmic movement and music as part of an involved and complex prayer ritual. The public dance is the culmination of weeks of less visible activity.*

K. C. DEN DOOVEN

PAUL VIGIL
'94
©

The casual observer often labels Indian dances and the accompanying music as "monotonous." It may well appear that way if one does not know the language and is unfamiliar with the music, but even a slightly alert visitor will soon realize that complicated rhythms and dance steps are employed and anyone who attempts to "keep the beat" will find himself confused by the frequent changes.

The moieties dance alternately during the day—both groups and their choruses then combine for a spectacular final performance at the end of the day.

## HUNTING CEREMONIALS

Hunting was formerly an important activity. Deer was the most common game animal but antelope, elk, and mountain sheep were also hunted for meat and hides. The Rio Grande Pueblo people ventured onto the Great Plains occasionally to hunt buffalo, a dangerous journey that exposed them to attack from hostile tribes who jealously guarded their territories against trespassers.

To be successful in hunting, a man had to have more than just practical skills—he also needed the cooperation of the animals he hunted, and it was to this end that most hunting rituals were directed. This was not a matter of a superior being attempting to control a lower life form, but one in which two equals sought an understanding of their respective roles in the scheme of life. As the cloven-hoofed mammals must eat plants to survive, so must man rely partly on animals, in turn, to sustain himself.

The hunting dances not only honored the animals, but also ensured their propagation. Further, they gained the cooperation and permission of the game so the hunters could take those that were needed for food and clothing.

Even today hunting requires rites before, during, and after the hunt. Fetishes are used in an effort to obtain assistance from the beasts of prey—the expert hunters of the animal world. If a hunter is successful, he first removes the heart from the game and ceremonially feeds it to his fetish. Tobacco, cornmeal, and a prayer feather may be offered to the dead animal's spirit to appease it and ensure it will return, thereby guaranteeing a steady supply of game animals.

Upon returning to the village the game is taken to the home of the hunter, wrapped in a ceremonial robe, and greeted as a visitor by those who enter the house. Anything less than this ritual treatment would offend the animals and the deity who is in charge of all game.

Respect for the animal continues even after it has been consumed. The skulls of deer and elk are painted with clay, and prayer feathers are hung from the antlers before they are placed on the housetop. During the animal dances, the homes bearing skulls are visited by the dancers. The bones of the animals are never thrown to the dogs, but are blessed with cornmeal and ceremonially deposited in the Rio Grande.

*A Pueblo animal dance with deer and mountain sheep. Tonita Peña*

## ANIMAL DANCES

Animal dances in the Rio Grande pueblos are usually winter ceremonials. The number of participants varies greatly and may include as few as a pair of Buffalo dancers and a Buffalo Woman, who represents the Mother of All Game, or a massed group of deer, elk, buffalo, antelope, and mountain sheep impersonators plus a hunt chief, hunters, a drummer, and chorus.

A typical Tewa animal ceremonial begins the night preceding the dance. Small fires are built in the plaza and on the housetops to guide the animals to the village. At dawn the Hunt Chief calls in the animals from the surrounding hills and leads them along paths of sacred cornmeal into the plaza where they dance. The impersonators often carry two sticks with which they imitate the movements of the forefeet of the animals.

In Keresan pueblos a young female participant races into the hills in the early morning where she "captures" the animal dancers and leads them to the village. The dance plaza is planted with small evergreens, and in this artificial forest the animal impersonators dance. At the end of the performance the hunters shoot the dancers with arrows of straw, and carry them off to their houses where they are honored as slain game. This ritual assures the success of the hunters when they go out after real game.

*In the Deer Dance, held at San Ildefonso Pueblo, the dancers use wooden staffs to represent the forelegs of the deer. The "legs" have evergreen attached to them to symbolize the deer's mountain home.*

Gilbert Atencio
60

AMERIND FOUNDATION, INC.

*The eagle is the most powerful of birds—able to fly out of sight into the clouds and believed to have a close relationship with the sun. The Eagle Dance honors the eagle and its role as an intermediary between humans and the sky deities. Gilbert Atencio*

## EAGLE DANCE

The eagle plays an important role in Pueblo mythology. A powerful bird, it can soar out of sight so it is believed to have a close relationship with the sun. Its power is often sought in curing rites, and its plumage is an essential part of many costumes of both masked and unmasked dancers. The downy feathers represent the "breath of life" and are used as prayer plumes by all tribes.

A favorite performance at public exhibitions, the Eagle Dance is also given in the villages. The ritual, performed by young men who imitate the eagles' flight, depicts man's affinity with the sky deities through the eagle as an intermediary. The dancers often wear a decorated shield on their backs. To some this indicates that the eagle is the chief of birds—others refer to the shield as a "moisture tablet," an acknowledgment of the eagle's ability to bring rain from the clouds it can soar through.

*Beginning at a very young age, children in many Rio Grande pueblos take part in Pueblo religious traditions, thereby learning their importance.*

## HOOP DANCE

The origin of the Hoop Dance is unknown, but there is some suggestion that it was originally a symbolic reenactment of man's emergence from the Underworld. Today it is staged at most public exhibitions and powwows as a spectacular acrobatic performance. The dancers are usually dressed in costumes of the Plains Indian variety.

*The Hoop Dance is a staple of most powwows and public performances. Though costumes are usually styled after the Plains Indians, many believe the dance may have originally symbolized Pueblo emergence legends. Guy Nez Jr.*

*Exposed to television, videos, and computers, Pueblo children are also exposed to ancient Pueblo traditions, which form the core of their identity and a part of their expression of daily life. Gina Chavarria*

# Zuni

The Zuni have probably the most complex of all native religions in the Southwest. Every aspect of traditional Zuni life is completely integrated with their religion. Numerous religious organizations, through an intricate system of interlocking ceremonials, interrelate the whole of Zuni culture.

Six esoteric cults (in addition to the ancestor cult to which all Zuni belong) form the basis of Zuni ceremonialism. These are the cults of the Sun, Rainmakers (which is in charge of 12 priesthoods), *Kokko* (or katsinas), Priests of the Kokko, War Gods, and Prey Gods (representing the animal patrons of 12 related curing societies). Each cult has its own priests, fetishes, rituals, and ceremonial calendar.

Basic to the religious philosophy of the Zuni is the recognition of man's oneness with the universe and the absolute necessity of maintaining this harmony through the correct execution of prescribed rituals. If the ceremonies are properly performed, the rains *will* fall, the harvests *will* be bountiful, the life of the people *will* be long and happy, and the fertility of the plant and animal worlds *will* continue.

### CREATION MYTH

In the beginning there was only fog and mists. "Above" existed three deities: *Awonawilona*—a bisexual supreme being (Creator of All); Sun, the giver of light, warmth, and life; and Moon, the deity responsible for dividing the year into 12 months and delineating the life span of man. "Below" existed two superhuman beings, *Shiwanni* and his wife *Shiwanokia*.

*The Zuni Shalako is the most typically Zuni image—in the non-Zuni mind, at least. These kokkos or spirit beings are not often carved at Zuni. One is more likely to see the image used in paintings or in their fine inlaid shell and turquoise jewelry.*

*The first part of the public portion of the Zuni Shalako ceremony begins with the sighting of them far to the south of the village. This is a re-enactment of the migrations of the* A:shiwi—*the Zuni people—that led them to their present home. Awa Tsireh*

Awonawilona created clouds and water with the breath of his heart. Shiwanni formed the constellations from bubbles of his saliva. Shiwanokia, using her saliva, created Mother Earth. The *A:shiwi* (Zuni) are the children of Shiwanni and Shiwanokia—they were born in the innermost of the underworlds.

EMERGENCE AND MIGRATION MYTH

The Underworld which the A:shiwi inhabited was totally dark—the people lived in holes and subsisted on wild grass seeds. They are said to have been peculiar creatures with tails, gigantic ears, webbed hands and feet, moss-covered bodies, and a foul odor.

Sun Father created two sons, *Kowituma* and *Wahtsusi*, out of bits of foam and sent them to the Underworld to bring the A:shiwi into the Upperworld. The sons, known as the Divine Ones, made light for the people by kindling fire. Following a path marked with sacred meal, they led the A:shiwi to the North where they planted a ponderosa pine. They climbed the tree to make their way into the Third or Water Moss World. The next trail led to the West—here a Douglas fir was grown to allow the A:shiwi to enter the Second or Mud World. The third trail went South to an aspen which was used to reach the First World of Wings (Sun's Rays). The last journey was to the East, and the A:shiwi climbed a silver spruce to emerge into the Upperworld. The actual entry was made through a spring or small lake whose waters parted to allow passage.

At the time of emergence the Divine Ones used their stone knives to transform the animal-like A:shiwi into human form. They also taught the Zuni how to make fire and to cook their food. Corn was acquired from *Paiyatemu*, assistant to the Sun.

The Zuni then began their wanderings to seek the Middle Place (the middle of the world) where they were to settle. Many years were spent

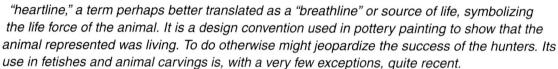

*Fetishes are objects, carved or in their natural state, which have a spirit inside that can assist the owner if treated with proper respect and ritual. This Zuni bear, carved of jet (a type of coal), is inlaid with a coral "heartline," a term perhaps better translated as a "breathline" or source of life, symbolizing the life force of the animal. It is a design convention used in pottery painting to show that the animal represented was living. To do otherwise might jeopardize the success of the hunters. Its use in fetishes and animal carvings is, with a very few exceptions, quite recent.*

in the search and numerous villages were built only to be later abandoned. At one stage in the wanderings Shiwanni of the North sent his son and daughter to seek a village site. During their search the brother suddenly became enamored of his sister's beauty and possessed her. The same night ten offspring were born to them—the first was normal and became the ancestor of the *Kokokshi*, the Rainmakers. The other nine became the *Koyemshi* (Mudheads), the idiot offspring of this incestuous union.

The brother created the Zuni and Little Colorado rivers by marking the sands with his foot, and at their junction a lake (Listening Spring) was formed. Within the waters of this lake he created a village, *Kothluwalawa* (sometimes called *Wenima*), the home of the Council of the Gods.

The Council of the Gods came into being as the result of a river crossing by the A:shiwi during their migration. The children of the Wood Fraternity were being carried across, but became panicky and fell into the rushing water. Immediately they were transformed into various water creatures—turtles, tadpoles, frogs, and snakes—which made their way to Kothluwalawa. Here they matured instantly and became the Council of the Gods.

In their migration to the Middle Place the A:shiwi were stopped by a tribe known as *Kianakwe*, which was led by *Chakwena*, the Keeper of the Game. The Divine Ones grew weary of leading the A:shiwi in fighting the Kianakwe, so they petitioned their Sun Father to send them two War Gods as replacements. The Sun impregnated a waterfall and the *Ahayuda* (as they are known in time of peace) or *Uyuyewi* and *Masailema* (as they are known in time of war) were created.

With the help of the War Gods the A:shiwi defeated the Kianakwe in a four-day battle. They captured the village and released the wild game held captive by Chakwena. The ruins of the village are said to be some 50 miles south of the present town of Zuni.

The A:shiwi continued to wander and lived in several villages (the ruins of which may still be seen) before they finally settled in the Middle Place, *Itiwanna*, the Zuni name for their pueblo.

## AFTERWORLD

At death the corpse is bathed in yucca suds and rubbed with cornmeal before burial. The spirit of the dead lingers for four days, during which time the door of its former home is left ajar to permit its entry. On the morning of the fifth day the spirit goes to the Council of the Gods in the village of Kothluwalawa beneath the water of Listening Spring. Here the spirit becomes a member of the *Uwannami*—a Rainmaker. If the deceased was a member of the Bow Priesthood, he becomes

Fetishes can be owned by individuals, clans, religious societies, or the tribe itself. Many of the more important communally owned ones may be kept in special bowls. This is a replica of such a bowl.

Though Hopi katsina ceremonies may be better known than Zuni kokko ceremonies, the Zuni's highly complex religious calendar is filled with rituals which involve some of the many Zuni kokko or spirit beings. J. Cachini

a lightning maker who brings water from the "six great waters of the world." The water, in the form of rain, is poured through the clouds which are the masks worn by the Uwannami.

## SHALAKO

The *Shalako*, a winter ceremony held in late November or early December, is the major ritual performed at the pueblo of Zuni. Usually referred to as a house-blessing ceremonial, it is a 49-day re-enactment of the Zuni emergence and migration myths. In addition, it is a prayer for rain, for the health and well-being of the people, and for the propagation of plants and animals. During the Shalako the spirits of the dead return to be honored and fed. As the final element of this lengthy ceremonial, a hunting rite is performed. The description that follows can do little more than touch the surface of this highly complex ceremonial.

Participants in the Shalako (both impersonators and the sponsors of the Shalako houses) are

chosen during the previous Winter Solstice ceremony. Preparations for the numerous and varied rites begin immediately afterward and occupy much of the participants' time for the intervening ten months. Long and complicated chants must be learned, prayer sticks must be placed each month at certain shrines that mark the migrations of the Zuni in ancient times, and minor rituals must be performed each month.

In addition to this, the houses that will honor the Shalakos must be built or extensively remodeled. (The floor is left unfinished and dug deep enough to accommodate the tall Shalakos.) Ideally, eight houses are used—six for the Shalakos, one for *Sayatasha* and the Council of the Gods (usually called the Long Horn House), and one for the *Koyemshi*. To sponsor a Shalako house is a tremendously expensive undertaking— added to the cost of construction is the expense of providing food for the participants and a myriad of visitors.

The principal masked figures that appear during the ceremony are:

*Shalakos*—the Giant Messengers of the Rainmakers—one to represent each of the six kivas. The masks and bodies of these ten-foot figures are carried on pole frames by the impersonators. Each Shalako has two impersonators who take turns dancing.

*Sayatasha*—the Rain God of the North—often called "Long Horn" for the projection from the right side of his mask which is said to symbolize long life for the people. Sayatasha oversees all the activities preceding the actual appearance of the Shalakos.

*Hututu*—the Rain God of the South—is the deputy of Sayatasha. Both carry rattles of deer scapulae, bows and arrows, and numerous prayer plumes.

*Shulawitsi*—the Fire God—is a representative of the sun. The part is always played by a young

*The Shalako ceremony is usually thought of as a house blessing. However, the 49-day observance includes a number of other aspects—re-enactment of the emergence and migrations of the Zuni people, prayer offerings to ensure the well-being of the people and the propagation of plants and animals, and a hunting rite. Mac Schweitzer*

boy from the Badger Clan. Shulawitsi carries a fawn skin filled with seeds.

*Yamuhakto*—Spirits of the Forest—these two figures are also called Warriors of the West and East. They have sticks of cottonwood tied to the tops of their masks that represent their authority over forests and trees. The antlers that they carry are symbolic of the deer that live in the forests.

*Salimopya*—are the warriors who carry yucca whips to guard the performers and keep spectators from coming too close. There are six—one for each of the six directions, with masks painted accordingly—but only two appear during the Shalako.

*Koyemshi*—the Mudheads—are led by *Awan Tachu*, Great Father. The others are called Deputy to the Great Father, Warrior, Bat, Small Horns, Old Grandfather, Old Youth, Water Drinker, Game Maker, and Small Mouth.

Members of the Council of the Gods taking part in this ceremony include Sayatasha, Hututu, two Yamuhakto, and Shulawitsi.

*(continued on page 34)*

*A model of a Zuni temporary shrine (as opposed to the permanent ones that dot Zuniland) with the masks of* Shulawitsi *and two* Salimopya— *Zuni warriors. There are six* Salimopya, *each colored to represent a different direction. Only two appear during Shalako.*

PHOTOS BY K. C. DEN DOOVEN

*Deposits of prayer offerings are an important part of the Shalako ceremony. On the final day the Shalako races take place. As the Shalako dancers race away, young men try to catch them to ensure luck in hunting deer. Mac Schweitzer*

Eight days before the arrival of the Shalakos, Koyemshi appear in the village to exhort the people to complete their preparations for the coming of the gods.

Four days later Shulawitsi and Sayatasha arrive from the west, having retraced the migration of the A:shiwi. The Fire God lights fires on the way to guide the Council of the Gods to the Middle Place.

## FORTY-EIGHTH DAY

Shulawitsi and Sayatasha appear in the village to inspect the six holes—one for each kiva—that have been dug to receive prayer plumes. Later in the day the Fire God and his ceremonial father deposit their prayer sticks. They are followed by Sayatasha, Hututu, and the two

*Preceding pages: Navajo come from afar to attend the summer Entah ceremony's Round Dance. Quincy Tahoma Photo from the Amerind Foundation, Inc.*

Yamuhakto who bless the shrines in brief ceremonies and also leave prayer plumes. They then retreat to their Shalako house to perform blessing ceremonies for the building and the altar that has been installed, and to place special prayer sticks near the roof beams. After this they smoke cigarettes of native tobacco. The smoke, symbolic of clouds, will bring rain to the land.

At dark the giant Shalakos arrive at the south side of the river where they use a narrow footbridge to cross over into the village. Upon reaching the north side the impersonators briefly leave their masks and go to the Shalako houses. They return shortly and the bird-like creatures rise and approach the houses with much clacking of beaks and strange whistling sounds. Before they enter, the houses must be properly blessed in ceremonies similar to those conducted at the Long Horn House.

After bringing the Shalako inside, the impersonator leaves his mask and enters into a lengthy dialogue with the sponsor of the houses. This recitation of the emergence and migration myth consumes a great part of the evening. Food is then taken by the Shalako impersonators to the

river where it is offered to the spirits of the dead who live at Kothluwalawa.

General feasting follows and the kitchens of the Shalako houses bring forth unbelievable quantities of food for performers, townspeople, and visitors.

Dancing by the Shakalos begins after midnight. The Salimopyas and Koyemshi also make the rounds to all of the Shalako houses to perform. A Zuni version of the Navajo Ye'ii Bichaii is also staged—to the great delight of the Navajos who are present. It is said that this dance commemorates a time when the Navajos performed this ceremony at Zuni to cure the people of an epidemic that caused swellings.

### FORTY-NINTH DAY

The dancing continues until sunrise, at which time Sayatasha climbs to a rooftop to offer prayers on behalf of the Zuni people. The dancers are purified with a hair-washing rite.

About noon on the final day, the Shalakos and their attendants leave the pueblo, crossing the river to an open field south of the old village. Here the Shalakos race, placing prayer plumes in six specially dug sites before returning to Kothluwalawa. The race depicts the manner in which the Shalakos, as couriers of the gods, deliver messages and prayers for rain throughout the year.

As the Shalakos disappear in the distance, the young men run to catch them. Those who succeed in "capturing" a Shalako believe they will have future success in hunting deer.

*Zuni fetishes include a group called* weh'mah'weh *or prey beings, like this bear with an arrow tied to its back.*

# Hopi Pueblos

### EMERGENCE MYTH

Each Hopi village has its own particular version of the emergence myth, and legends that trace the wanderings of the Hopis before they reached their present location vary with each clan.

*Huru'ing Wuuhti* (in some legends it is Spiderwoman) is credited with creating mankind out of saliva and colored sand. Four sets of male and female figures, black, red, yellow, and white, were made. Each was given a different language and the power to reproduce. Life began in the innermost of four Underworlds. Some legends depict life there as good, with animals and people living in harmony and amidst plenty. Others maintain the Underworlds were dark and overcrowded, and that the upward journey was an attempt to alleviate those unpleasant conditions.

Most of the stories allude to social disorder caused by the presence of *powaku* or witches. The dissension and fighting that followed caused the people to forget their ceremonies and life plan. In disgust, *Sotunangu* (God of the Sky) destroyed, in turn, each Underworld in an attempt to wipe out the witches and related failure to live right. Each time a few good people were saved to populate the new world only to repeat the mistakes of the previous one.

To escape the flood that was used to destroy the Third Underworld, the priests sought the aid of animals and birds. They had heard the footsteps of someone walking above and decided to ask permission to ascend to the next world.

After several attempts by different birds, the shrike found the opening that led to the Upperworld. To reach the *Sipapu*, the Place of Emergence, the help of the chipmunk was sought. Chipmunk planted a series of trees and sang magic songs over them in an effort to make them grow tall enough to reach the opening discovered by the shrike. Neither the spruce nor the pine trees grew tall enough, but a bamboo finally grew up through the hole. Chipmunk then chewed an opening at the base of the reed to admit the passage of the people.

The One Horned priests stayed below to prevent the witches from reaching the Upperworld. Before all the people had reached the Sipapu they cut down the reed. The joints in the bamboo were caused by the people who were trapped inside. Despite the precautions, some witches succeeded in reaching the new world. Another version describes a raft constructed of reeds that the people used to ride out the flood.

For roughly six months out of the year, the katsinas visit the Hopi people and assist in the performance of religious ceremonies meant to ensure the renewal of the cycle of life for all living beings—plants, animals, and people. Ray Naha

At the time of emergence this world was occupied only by *Masau'u*, a deity. According to some versions, Masau'u himself assisted the people through the Sipapu. In others, the first contact with Masau'u was made by the shrike, who acted as an intermediary. In any case, Masau'u gave the Hopis permission to settle in his land and marked off the boundaries of the territory they were to occupy.

## AFTERWORLD

At death the hair of the deceased is washed in yucca suds, and prayer feathers are placed on the body before burial. Those involved in the burial are later purified with juniper smoke.

The ghosts or spirits of the dead are feared rather than death itself. To prevent the spirits from returning to bother the living, *pahos,* or prayer offerings, are given to the parting spirit of the deceased and the trail back to the village is ceremonially closed with cornmeal.

The spirits of those who have done their best to behave well during their lives reach the village of the Cloud People and become cloud people themselves. Those who deliberately cause harm in their lives meet their ends in fire pits where they are thrown, later to emerge as black beetles.

The spirits of children who die before they are initiated into one of the Hopi religious societies are believed to return to the mother's house to be born again.

## PRINCIPAL DEITIES

The Hopi pantheon includes between 30 and 40 deities ranging in importance from culture heroes to major gods. There are often considerable differences in the functions and appearances of these deities among the various Hopi villages. The myths relating to the gods are sometimes vague, and may differ greatly from one mesa to the next.

*Sotunangu,* the God of the Sky, is considered by most Hopis to be the most important deity. Some refer to him as the Supreme Being, although he exercises no control over the other deities except for the Twin War Gods. Others call him Creator of the Earth for, according to one myth, he created a young maiden whom he later transformed into the earth. He is in charge of the heavens, lightning, and clouds, and can send rain to make the plants grow.

*Masau'u* is both the God of Earth and God of the Underworld. It was Masau'u who permitted the Hopi to settle in his domain. He is depicted as a giant of a man and black in color. Although believed to be handsome, he always wears a terrifying mask, covered with blood, whenever he has contact with people. He is thought of as a fertility god of man and animals and is also associated with fire.

*Mui'ingwa* or *Alosaka,* the God of Germination, is also called the Two-Horn or Germ God. Alosaka lives underground and is concerned primarily with the propagation

Hopi gourd rattles may be painted in a wide range of designs, but all have painted "stitching" around the perimeter, reminiscent of the ancient rawhide rattles that preceded them.

of plant life. He is thought by some to be responsible for the fertility of the sky and earth. His female counterpart, Sand Altar Woman, is associated with childbirth. Both were created by Huru'ing Wuuhti.

*Huru'ing Wuuhti* is thought of as the Mother of the Universe. As Goddess of Hard Substances (turquoise, shell, and coral) she is associated with wealth. Ugly by day and beautiful by night, she is visited daily by the Sun in her kiva which is located in the western ocean. She is credited most frequently with being the Creator of the World, and is said to own the stars and the moon.

*Kwanitaka* is the One Horned God who guards the entrance to the Underworld, and determines which trail the spirits of the dead will follow to reach the land of the Cloud People.

*Tawa,* the Sun or Father Sun, is thought of as the Giver of Life who acts as a special emissary for Sotunangu. Tawa travels daily to visit Huru'ing Wuuhti. The Sun has special powers that may be sought in ceremonials relating to

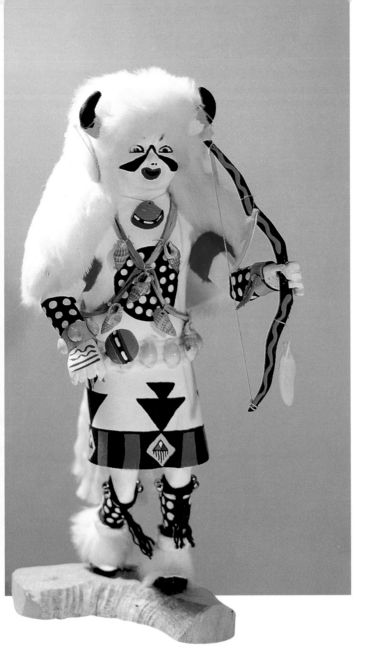

ing and preventing Palolokon from causing earthquakes. They are helpful to the Hopi people, but are not above playing tricks on them on occasion.

*Palolokon*, the Water Serpent, is probably related to the Plumed Serpent, *Quetzcoatl*, of the Aztecs. It is believed to inhabit the waters under the earth, and uses springs and lakes as windows to watch the people. When displeased it may cause floods and earthquakes, so this deity is one that must be placated. All moisture—sap, blood, and water—is in Palolokon's control.

*Mu'yao*, the Moon Deity, is seen as an old man who provides light at night. In the emergence legend Spiderwoman made the moon by weaving a white cotton robe and then placing it in the sky.

*Ong Wuuhti*, Salt Woman, inhabits the Salt Lake south of Zuni. Pahos are offered to her by Hopis who journey there to gather salt.

### KATSINAS

Katsinas are not gods, but the symbolic representation, in humanlike form, of the spirits of plants, animals, birds, places, ancestors, or forces of nature.

Katsinas at one time lived with the Hopis after their emergence from the Underworld and brought them rain with their dances, but the people became disrespectful so the katsinas left them and went off to live by themselves. Before they departed, however, they agreed to teach the people how to perform their rituals.

A katsina impersonator is believed to receive the spirit of the katsina he depicts when he wears the mask. (The mask, though sacred, does not actually house the spirit.) In doing so he straddles the threshold between the world of the Hopi people and the katsina world, enabling him to act as an intermediary, conveying the prayers of the Hopi people to the deities.

Classifying katsinas is a pastime of students of Pueblo religion, but not of the Indians themselves. They find classifying and counting to be of

both war and fertility. A morning prayer and an offering of cornmeal are made to the Sun daily by traditional Hopis. Newborn children are "presented" to the sun on the eighth day. Tawa is especially honored at the Winter Solstice ceremony to bring him back from his northward journey.

*Kokyang Wuuhti*, Spiderwoman, is depicted as a wise, kind old woman who is always ready to help the Hopi people. Each village has a shrine to this deity who is believed to be present everywhere. She is the mother of the Twin War Gods. In some legends Spiderwoman plays a major role in creating mankind—in others she is thought of as the creator only of those who are not Hopi.

*Po'okang Hoya* and *Palo'ngao Hoya* are the Twin War Gods created by Spiderwoman who is their grandmother. According to some legends they are responsible for keeping the world turn-

*Two very vital Hopi ceremonies are observed in winter. The renewal of the cycle of life is the focus of the Wuwutsim ceremony, when prayers are made for the germination of all forms of life. A new fire is kindled and distributed to each Hopi household. The other winter ceremony is the* Soyal, *held on the solstice. It marks the southernmost point of the sun's journey—the point at which it begins to return, ensuring that life will continue. Careful prayer offerings and rituals are absolutely crucial to the success of these ceremonies.*
*Milland Lomakema*

no more importance to the practice or understanding of their religion than Christians would find a similar pigeonholing of their numerous saints.

All Pueblo tribes have katsinas and related ceremonies, but the Hopi and the Zuni have the largest number. The Hopis have about 30 *mong* or "chief" katsinas who perform specific annual ceremonies. In addition to these there are over 200 other katsinas who may appear at various times during the katsina ceremonial year. Katsinas may be added or disappear depending upon need and effectiveness.

### KATSINA DANCES

Katsina dances are held outdoors in village plazas after the weather becomes milder, usually in April. Permission to stage a dance is given by the village chief; the sponsor of the dance determines which katsina will be presented and the day of the performance. Much time is spent by the impersonators in learning the songs that will be sung in the day-long presentation, and in preparing the masks and other necessary equipment.

The purpose of a katsina dance is multifold— the bringing of clouds and rain is of prime importance, but a successful dance also promotes harmony in the universe and ensures health, long life, and happiness for the people. It is believed that the prayers of the people will be conveyed by the katsinas to the gods.

## Major Ceremonies
### WUWUTSIM

*Wuwutsim* is an annual initiation ceremony in which the Emergence from the Underworld is reenacted. During the rites all trails and roads into the village are ceremonially closed with sacred cornmeal except the one leading from the burial ground. Lights and fires are extinguished and the spirits of the dead are invited to return to their villages. Masau'u officiates at the initiation and ceremonially kindles a new fire that is then distributed to all households in the village. No outside visitors are permitted to attend the Wuwutsim which is held in November.

### SOYAL

Shortly after the Wuwutsim the *Soyal* katsina appears in the village. His walk is unsteady and he sings in a quiet voice. Some believe this is because he has just awakened from a prolonged sleep. Others say the halting movements are childlike and symbolic of being reborn.

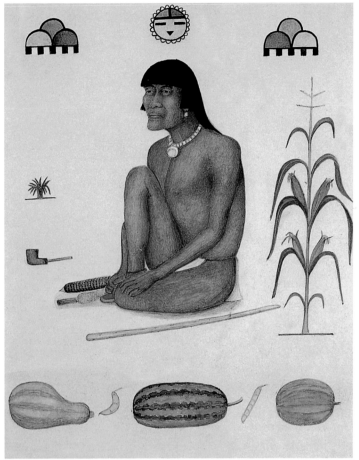

AMERIND FOUNDATION, INC.

Soyal is the Winter Solstice ceremony held in December. The main purpose of the ceremony is to bring back the sun from its northward journey. It is also a time for purification and blessing rites to mark the rebirth of another year. Numerous pahos are made during the Soyal for houses, animals, plants, people, and objects. It is during this time that the kivas are ritually opened to mark the beginning of the katsina ceremonial year.

## POWAMU

*Powamu*, commonly called the Bean Dance, is the first major ceremony of the new year and includes the appearance of a number of *mong* katsinas. (Prior to this, night dances have been held in the kivas.) It is at this ceremony that the greatest variety and number of katsina dancers participate. Beans are planted in boxes of moist sand and forced to grow in the kivas where constant fires create a hothouse atmosphere.

An initiation for children into either the Powamu or Katsina society is also performed during the 16-day Powamu ceremony. The children are ritually whipped, and afterwards learn that the katsina dancers are impersonated by humans.

The Powamu dancers perform in the kiva to bless the bean sprouts. If the beans have grown tall, a good harvest is predicted for the coming summer. Early the following morning the bean sprouts are distributed throughout the village, and the children receive presents—basketry plaques, katsina dolls, bows and arrows, rattles, moccasins—from the katsinas.

Powamu is also a time for the *Soyoko* katsinas to visit the homes of naughty children. These ugly monsters threaten to carry off and eat the disobedient youngsters if their behavior does not improve. The parents often must ransom the children with food. The sight of these terrifying ogres is enough to make anyone, young or old, improve his conduct.

## PACHAVU

Every four years *Pachavu* is held during Powamu. The observance includes a spectacular procession in which innumerable beautifully dressed katsinas appear, many carrying huge basketry plaques covered with bean sprouts. As the procession moves about the village it is joined by new katsinas, each singing his own song and dancing his particular steps.

## PALOLOKONTI

*Palolokonti* or the Water Serpent Ceremony (not an annual occurrence) takes place at night in the kiva about the same time as Powamu. The light is extinguished as the impersonators approach the kiva—in a matter of minutes the room is once again illuminated to reveal an elaborate screen that stretches nearly wall to wall. On the floor, in front of sun shield covers on the screen, are placed tiny corn shoots set in cones of clay. To the accompaniment of roaring sounds the sun shields lift and the heads of huge plumed and horned serpents appear. Snake-like, they sway farther and farther into the room while the Koyemsi (Mudheads) sing. With violent motions they sweep away the miniature cornfield.

*Hahai Wuuhti*, the Mother of all Katsinas, approaches the serpents with a tray of cornmeal and "nurses" each serpent. The Mudheads then attempt to push the serpents back under the sun shields, but the snakes resist. The action and the roaring increase in intensity as the

Mudheads wrestle with the Palolokon. The serpent figures give the impression of having tremendous strength, sending the Koyemsi tumbling. Finally, the serpents are forced back and the shields are closed—the kiva is darkened momentarily while the screen is dismantled and the performers depart.

The purpose of the Water Serpent Ceremony is to honor the giant reptiles who control the waters of the earth. If the unpredictable creatures can be placated the people will receive the moisture they need for their crops, and the springs, upon which the villages depend, will not fail.

## NIMAN

*Niman*, or Home Dance, is a 16-day ceremonial that begins shortly before the summer solstice and ends in mid-July. The dance held then marks the final religious observance of the katsina ceremonial year, and the katsinas return to their homes on *Nuva'tukya'ovi*, Snow Mountain (the San Francisco Peaks near Flagstaff, Arizona), until the next Soyal.

Almost any katsina may be impersonated at the Niman, but the *Hemis*, with its elaborate tablita, is usually the preferred one. The dance follows the usual form, but between each round the katsinas distribute gifts to those present.

Clowns (*Koyemsi, Koshare*, or *Tsuku*) appear to entertain the spectators with skits and games, often ribald in nature. Always the source of great amusement, they sometimes mimic the antics of non-Hopi or villagers whose behavior has not been proper.

Since the Niman coincides with the early harvest, corn and melons are distributed to the villagers and spectators. Bread, piki, and native foods are also tossed to the crowd. Children receive gifts of rattles, baskets, dolls, and bows and arrows, as well as cattails, which are chewed like gum. Captive eagles, kept on rooftops, also receive similar gifts.

The day after the Niman Dance the kivas are ritually closed and the eagles, which have been held captive since early spring, are "sent home"—smothered in sacred cornmeal. (Most tribes believe that the spirit of an animal killed and treated with respect will return in animal form again.) The feathers are removed for a variety of religious uses, and the bodies are buried with the same attention and ceremony that is given to deceased members of the tribe.

## FLUTE CEREMONY

The Flute Ceremony is performed biennially by the Gray Flute and Blue Flute societies. The usual explanation for the ritual is that it brings the late summer rains that are needed for the crops to reach full maturity. The ceremony is much more complex than this, however, for in addition to the rain-bringing function (which is a part of almost every ceremonial performed by the Pueblo Indians), the Flute ritual is a reenactment of the emergence and migration myths.

During the 16-day ceremonial, elaborate Flute altars are set up in the clan houses (rather than the kivas) and initiation rites for new society members are held. An important part of the ritual

Koshares, *black-and-white-striped Tewa clowns, help in a ceremony performed by male and female* Anak'tsina *or Long Hair katsinas, who are associated with the gentler summer rains that are vital to maturing crops in the arid Hopi homeland. A. A. Naha*

is a commemoration of the creation of the sun, and the participants in the public performance wear sun shields on their backs. On the sixteenth day, spectators may attend the final rites, which begin with the blessing of the village spring. Then the Gray Flute Society, followed by the Blue Flute Society, proceed to the village. Each is led by a priest and two Flute Maidens who carry small reed rings on slender rods.

On the way to the plaza the leader uses corn-meal to draw a cloud symbol on the ground, and the Flute Maidens, using the rods, toss the rings onto them—an act symbolic of the migrations (and stops along the way) of the Hopis. In some villages this rite is performed in the plaza.

When both societies are assembled in the plaza, the Gray Flute leader and his water carrier enter the *kisi* (a temporary shelter of cottonwood branches) to pray while the songs of the Emergence are sung by the chorus to the sound of reed flutes. At the end of the prayers, water from the water carrier's gourd is poured into the sym-bolic sipapu in the plaza. The Blue Flute leader and his assistant then enter the kisi and offer more prayers, and the ceremony ends after they emerge.

The flute is used in this ceremony to imitate the sound of cicadas, an insect associated with summer, since warm days and rain are needed to mature the crops. It is an attempt to prolong the summer growing season.

## SNAKE DANCE

Alternating with the biennial Flute Ceremony is the *Tsuh Tikive* or Snake Dance, the most widely known of all Hopi ceremonies. Although it is one of the Hopi rituals of lesser importance, it has historically drawn huge, ever-increasing crowds made up largely of curiosity seekers who are fascinated by the idea of seeing the dancers handle live, often poiso-nous snakes. The overwhelming number of spectators has forced the Hopis to close this ceremony to outsiders.

A 16-day ceremonial like the Flute Ceremony, the Snake Dance is believed to be one of the more ancient of Pueblo rituals. There is evidence that this ceremony was once per-formed in most of the Rio Grande pueblos in pre-Spanish times. Today it survives only in the Hopi villages.

The ceremony itself is based on a legend concerning a young Hopi man who attempted to find the source of all waters by following the Colorado River to its source. In a journey fraught with dangers he was assisted by Spiderwoman.

Eventually he met the Great Snake who con-trolled the waters of the world from his kiva. The young man was initiated into the Snake Tribe and was taught their ceremonies. Before he re-turned to his own people he married a young

# Apache

The Apache, who share a common linguistic and cultural background with the Navajo, also share similar religious beliefs and ceremonies (some of which are adapted from the Pueblo tribes). Curing rituals and blessing rites that include, among other things, the use of sandpaintings, make up the bulk of Apache ceremonialism. As a general rule, however, the Apache have fewer ceremonies and these tend to be less complex than those of the Navajo.

Mask worn by the Gaan *or Mountain Spirit Dancers of the Apache people.*

## DEITIES

*Ysun*, a supernatural force identified neither by sex nor location, is the Creator of the Universe and looked upon as the Supreme Being. Referred to as "The Giver of Life," Ysun is the source of all power and has great influence over the affairs of people.

Everything on the earth, animate or inanimate, and in the sky is believed to have a spirit—the sun, moon, thunder, wind, and lightning are especially powerful. Thunder Beings once lived with the people and served as hunters by killing game with flint-tipped shafts of lightning. The earth itself is often referred to as Earth Woman but it is not personified.

Changing Woman existed "from the beginning" and is the most important female deity. Born-of-Water and Monster Slayer, whose mythological exploits are similar to those of the Navajo Twin War Gods, are also important supernatural figures. They are the children of White Shell Woman.

White Shell Woman (or White Painted Woman, as she is sometimes called) and Changing Woman are closely associated with one another, but the exact relationship is not consistent among various Apache bands. Similarly, Born-of-Water and Monster Slayer may be identified as sons, husbands, or brothers of White Shell Woman. In one version of the creation myth, Born-of-Water is described as creating humans of mud or clouds, but generally Monster Slayer is regarded as the most important figure after Ysun.

A lesser but still important category of supernatural beings includes the Mountain People and Water People. The latter is made up of He Who Controls Water, a being who is dressed in a shirt of colored clouds and is responsible for the rains, and Water Monster, an unpleasant creature in serpent or human form which inhabits lakes and springs and causes the drowning of people and animals.

The Mountain People are the more important beings in this grouping. Called *Gaan* (and similar to the Navajo *ye'ii* or Hopi *Katsina*) these supernaturals are identified with the specific mountaintops and caves that they inhabit. Like the Thunder Beings they too once lived with ordinary people but, wishing to avoid the death that humans must eventually face, they left to seek a world of eternal life.

Coyote, in his usual role as troublemaker, is held responsible for bringing to man such undesirable things as death, gluttony, thievery, adultery, and lying. Among a few Apache bands, however, Coyote was credited with teaching people how to weave baskets, tan hides, and prepare various foods—but then had to be banished from the camps for his thievery.

### MOUNTAIN SPIRIT DANCE

Today the most important and elaborate ceremony given by the Apache is the girls' puberty rite. It is the only one they still have in common

*The* Gaan *traditionally appeared during times of impending disaster among the Apache people. They appear now only during the* Nah'ih'es *or coming-of-age ceremonies of Apache young women. They prevent any evil from disrupting the proceedings and possess power to cure by blowing away sickness. Ray Naha*

In Apache religion, one gains religious power through visions or dreams. The test of that power or the truth of the dream comes in the success (or failure) of the shaman—who may be a man or a woman. *Delmar Boni*

with their Athabascan-speaking relatives in Canada. According to their mythology it was White Shell Woman who taught this important ritual to the Apaches, and it is she with whom the young women identify during this annual summer ceremony.

Coming-of-age ceremonies are expensive affairs anywhere, and Apache society is no exception. The family of the young woman must hire a shaman (either male or female) to conduct the ceremony, provide payment for the Gaan dancers, and furnish huge quantities of food for the large number of friends, family, and visitors who will gather to attend the rituals and take part in the related social events.

On the first day a tipi frame is constructed of four spruce saplings to house the young girl and her older female attendant. The girl is dressed in ceremonial garments made of buckskin that have been painted yellow, the color of sacred pollen. The costume is a duplicate of the one worn by White Shell Woman, decorated with symbols of the moon, sun, and stars. The long fringe represents sunbeams.

The girl is believed to possess special curative powers at this time of her life, and may treat the sick and afflicted by touching or massaging.

Between the lengthy chants sung by the shaman (during which the girl dances on a buckskin) she attends all who come to her for aid.

Many taboos must be observed by the young lady, for her future depends on her disposition and deportment during the four-day ritual. She is cautioned against smiling or laughing because this would result in premature wrinkling. The ceremonial is symbolic of the life journey the girl will take. If all goes well she will enjoy a long, happy, and healthful life on the "pollen path."

On each of the four nights, impersonators of the Gaan—Mountain Spirits—will perform to bless the encampment and drive away any evil that may disrupt the proceedings. During this time the Mountain Spirit Dancers (often incorrectly referred to as Crown or Devil Dancers) also possess powers to cure and may treat patients by blowing away the sickness. The Gaan are popular with the Apache, and there is much rivalry among dance groups. In early times the Gaan

*Central to the Apache creation story, depicted here by Yavapai-Apache artist Duke Sine, is Changing Woman, believed by many to represent the Earth itself. Her child, Born-of-Water (below) joined with Monster Slayer (right) to rid the earth of monsters, making it safe for the humans who would follow. To the left are the Gaan or Mountain Spirits—guardians of the Apache people. The game animals are at right, while animals not meant to be hunted for food are at left—including Coyote, who stole fire for the humans. The hummingbirds at each corner are messengers carrying the news that the Apache people have emerged.*

dancers often appeared to protect the bands from impending disasters such as epidemics. Now their appearances are limited to puberty rites and public exhibitions.

The dancers, who may number anywhere from 4 to 16 plus 1 or more clowns, are painted under the direction of the shaman. At dusk they enter the dance ground, first approaching both the central fire and ceremonial tipi four times as a blessing.

A chorus, which carries the refrain to the verses sung by the medicine man, and a drummer accompany the dancers. The song determines which dance step will be used—short, high, or free. Aside from the basic step restriction, each dancer performs as an individual. The dance itself is characterized by short, jerky, angular movements, and much posturing and gesturing with painted swordlike wands of yucca.

The dancers perform at intervals throughout each night. In between times the crowd participates in Round Dances—a form of social dancing identical with the Round Dance of the Navajo.

At the end of four days the tipi is ceremonially dismantled and the visitors depart. The family remains at the campground until the ninth day, on which the girl is purified by a bath in yucca suds. She then assumes the role of a marriageable woman.

# Tohono O'odham

While there is considerable doubt—among both tribal elders and archaeologists—as to how closely related the ancient Hohokam and the Tohono O'odham are, Hohokam motifs are sometimes utilized by tribal artists.

## ORIGIN MYTH

The origin myth, which takes an experienced storyteller four nights to complete, varies considerably in detail among the four dialect divisions of the Tohono O'odham. The version given here, which shares some similarities with Pueblo emergence legends, is a mere outline of the full story.

In the beginning there was only a darkness in which Earthmaker and Buzzard drifted.

Earthmaker rubbed dirt from his skin and held it in his hand—out of it grew a greasewood (creosote) bush. From a ball of gum taken from the creosote Earthmaker then created the world. As the earth was being joined to the sky, *I'itoi*, another supernatural, came into being. *Coyote*, who served as a messenger for the deities, also appeared about the same time.

The newly formed universe was a wobbly affair until the Spider People sewed the earth and sky together. Buzzard formed the water courses with his wing tips, and Earthmaker created the stars, sun, and moon.

The first attempt to create human life resulted in imperfect beings, so the supernaturals brought about a flood to destroy them. Before the flood Earthmaker, I'itoi, and Coyote agreed among themselves that the first of them to appear afterwards would be known as Elder Brother. I'itoi emerged first and assumed the title.

Elder Brother then formed new human beings from clay, but this led to a conflict with Earthmaker who angrily disappeared underground where he lives today.

I'itoi dwelt with his creations (identified as the ancient Hohokam), and taught them how to live in the desert and gave them ceremonies necessary to bring rain. Hostility between I'itoi and the people broke out, and they decided to kill him. In four years I'itoi revived with the help of the winds, and then went underground to secure aid from the people there. These were the Pima and Tohono O'odham and they agreed to help I'itoi.

In this extremely dry land, "life-giving water" is more than an idle phrase. As evidenced by these large, well-formed water jars, the O'odham treat it preciously.

Gopher burrowed through the ground to lead the people out of the four Underworlds. With I'itoi's assistance they drove out the Hohokam. I'itoi then helped the Pima and Tohono O'odham establish themselves in the desert. In one version he explained that he was giving the Tohono O'odham the arid desert because only they, of all peoples, could survive there. The boundaries for each group were marked by corn kernels carried by the winds. I'itoi then left and returned to live underground in the vicinity of Baboquivari Peak.

## CURING RITES

Most human disease is believed to be caused by animals that have been injured or otherwise treated disrespectfully. Medicine men called *makahs* have the power to diagnose the cause, and the patient then goes to a singer who possesses the power and fetishes to effect a cure.

Rattlesnakes can cause stomach aches—sore feet might be caused by a horned lizard. Offending a turtle could result in a crippled leg, and a deer that had been left wounded could bring rheumatism. Each malady requires a series of songs to cure it. In case the disease is traced to an animal introduced by the Spaniards, it might be necessary to recite a rosary.

## AFTERWORLD

Disposal of the corpse took place soon after death, as the ghosts of the deceased were greatly feared. Formerly burial was made in a rock crevice and covered with stones, or in a stone cairn roofed with wood. Food and possessions were placed with the body in the grave to accompany the spirit on its four-day journey to the Underworld in the East. The afterworld was believed to be a place of much rain and plenty of food.

*In small villages scattered in the vastness of the Sonoran Desert can be found large ramadas in front of traditional Rain Houses where ceremonies like the* Wi:gida *are held. While most ceremonies held in public were traditionally open to attendance by Indian and non-Indian alike, the desire of non-Indians to know every detail, down to the most secret (and therefore most powerful) aspect, combined with the problem of sheer numbers, has forced many tribes to become more protective of their traditions.*

Today, annual offerings of food and drink are made at graves of the deceased on All Souls Day, a practice borrowed from the Mexicans, but not unlike the native custom.

## TOHONO O'ODHAM CEREMONIES

Although most Tohono O'odham have long been converted to various Christian sects, a number of the old ceremonials are still performed.

Tohono O'odham ceremonialism is a mixture of hunting and agricultural rituals. The most important aspect of each rite is the bringing of life-sustaining rain to the land. Any successfully conducted ritual (inter-village races and games, salt pilgrimages to the Sea of Cortez, dances, curing and puberty rites, as well as ceremonies performed at local shrines) can bring rain.

*Though rarely seen by non-Tohono O'odham, the* Wi:gida, *a harvest ceremony, is still held. The recent publication of a 50-year-old description of this ceremony caused a controversy because of the tribe's desire to protect its traditions. Mike Chiago*

### SAGUARO WINE FESTIVAL

Late in June, when the fruit of the giant saguaro cactus ripens, the Tohono O'odham conduct a ceremony to celebrate what is essentially the beginning of the new year. The period just before the saguaro harvest was one of starvation, for neither cultivated nor wild crops were available yet and last year's provisions were usually gone. It was once the custom to take the first ripened saguaro fruit one found and hold it over one's heart and breathe a silent prayer of thanksgiving.

This particular ceremony, called the *Nawait*, was taught them by I'itoi. According to one version, they had to hold the ceremony in order to convince Wind and Rain to return after an absence of several years. The saguaro, which produces fresh fruit, syrup, and a meal made from the seeds, can also produce a wine—from the fermented syrup.

The syrup-making process produces a juice that is allowed to ferment for three days in the Rain House, under the care of the Keeper of the Smoke, who is the village headman and ceremonial leader. Rain songs are sung while the liquid ferments, and the men and women—who once painted their torsos with butterfly designs—dance at night. As a part of the fertility ritual, sexual license was permitted at this time.

At noon on the third day, the headmen gathered to recite long poems over the baskets of wine. The men of the village sat in a circle and passed the baskets around until they were drained. The drinking of wine, like the smoking of tobacco, was considered a ceremonial duty and was not indulged in for mere pleasure.

The planting of crops takes place after the wine festival to make use of the rains that are bound to follow.

*The* Corso de Gallo *or Chicken Pull is a ritual that has rainmaking significance and is usually held on San Juan's Day (June 24), locally thought of as the first day of the summer rains. Leonard Chana*

Today, some families also prepare saguaro wine for their own use at this time, but the custom to "cover the wine with a song" continues and anyone who accepts a drink of the liquor must recite a poem relating to clouds and rains.

### TCIRKWENA DANCE

It used to be customary for villages to challenge one another to games, contests, or dances. One such dance is the *Tcirkwena*, referred to variously as a Skipping Dance, Season Dance, or Winter Rain Dance.

The series of eight songs required for these dances were dreamed by a singer. This man would then train young boys and girls to perform the dance steps. During the dance they carry effigies of birds, clouds, or rainbows made of cotton.

Musical accompaniment is provided by basket drums, rasps, and a chorus of older men (or women, today) who had learned the song series.

The village that hosts the dancers considers the ceremony as a blessing which assures them of sufficient rainfall. The older women of the village might honor the visitors by dancing alongside them. After the performance, guests are given a feast and gifts in payment.

### CHICKEN PULL

*Corso de Gallo,* or the Chicken Pull, is a game that was introduced into the Southwest along with the horse by the Spaniards. It is a contest of riding skill, traditionally performed on San Juan's Day (June 24), though it may be held at other times as a separate event or in connection with a native ceremonial.

The Tohono O'odham version of the Chicken Pull takes place on a sandy racetrack several hundred feet long. Halfway down the track a live rooster is buried up to its neck in the loose sand. Individual riders galloping past lean far out of their saddles and attempt to pull the rooster out of the ground. The rooster frantically tries to dodge the grasping fingers, and it usually takes many tries before a rider succeeds in wrenching the luckless fowl free.

A general free-for-all follows with all riders trying to grab the rooster and the successful contestant beating off the attackers by swinging the rooster at them.

Most tribes that adopted the Chicken Pull have given it some religious connotation. Among the Rio Grande pueblos it has an agricultural significance with the "planting" and subsequent removal of the rooster as symbolic of sowing and reaping. The blood and feathers of the fowl and the foam and sweat of the lathered horses represent rain and clouds, and are considered to be a blessing for the earth, promoting fertility.

Among the Tohono O'odham the rainmaking significance was probably the main consideration, for locally San Juan's Day is still traditionally thought of as a day of rain—often the first of summer.

# Yaqui

The Yaqui world is called *Huiya Ania,* and within that world exists the *Seah Ania* or Flower World, which then contains the *Yo Ania* or Enchanted World where many of the spirits or spiritual forces reside. Then comes the *Tuka Ania* or Night World which includes all types of night phenomena and finally, within that, the *Tenka Ania* or Dream World, which is the source of dreams for the individual.

Yaqui legend tells of a time when there appeared a tree that spoke, but in a strange language none knew. Many came but no one could understand its words. Finally, two daughters of an old man came and listened and were able to translate. The Talking Tree prophesied the coming of Christianity, loss of lands, war and even, some say, drug abuse problems.

The Yaquis' native religion was greatly changed by the introduction of Catholicism by Jesuit missionaries in the early 1600s. As enthusiastic converts, they soon observed a full Roman Catholic ceremonial calendar. Church rituals were not led by ordained priests, but by Yaqui men known as *maestros* (from Spanish for "teacher") who conducted services in a combination of Spanish, Yaqui, and Latin. Even today the Yaqui churches are totally independent of the Roman Catholic Church.

ARIZONA STATE MUSEUM

*The Yaqui Deer Dance is an ancient hunting ritual which has been incorporated into their observance of the Catholic Easter ceremony.*

## EASTER SEASON

The most elaborate ceremonies conducted in the Yaqui settlements of southern Arizona occur during Lent. These include the Yaqui version of the Catholic liturgy for the Lenten season and Easter, and a Passion play. The basic theme presented is the triumph of good over evil.

The *Fariseo* (Pharisees) and *Caballero* societies are in charge of the Easter ceremony. Their members impersonate the enemies of Christ who pursued and persecuted Him. *Chapayekas,* the common soldiers of the Fariseos, wear grotesque masks of painted hide or paper, and carry painted wooden swords and daggers. To prevent the evil he depicts from entering his heart, each Chapayeka must carry the cross of his rosary in his mouth while wearing the mask. The masks have no eyeholes, and can be taken off only when the mask is touching the ground.

The *Matachine* society is a men's dance group under vow to Mary, and is referred to as "soldiers of the Virgin." During the Easter ceremonies they are allied with the church group, led by the maestros, in opposition to the Fariseos. They wear headdresses decorated with paper flowers and ribbons, and carry wands decorated with brightly colored feathers. The young boys wear white dresses and act as guardians of the Virgin. The dances this group performs, including a maypole dance, all appear to be of European origin.

*The* Chapayekas *represent the soldiers of the* Fariseos *(Pharisees) in the Yaqui Easter ceremony. When they attack the church on Holy Saturday, the* Matachines *successfully defend it, "killing" the Chapayekas with flowers. Later, a figure of Judas is burned along with all the masks and equipment of the Chapayekas in order to purify the village of the evil they have absorbed.*

On Holy Saturday, the Matachines successfully defend the church against attack by the Fariseos and "kill" the Chapayekas with a barrage of flowers. (Flowers play an important part in Yaqui ceremonies—they represent divine blessings, a state of holiness, and a protection against evil.) The masks and equipment of the Chapayekas are later burned on a pyre along with a figure of Judas.

*A feather wand and rattle are carried by each Matachine dancer during part of the Easter ceremonies. The Matachines are the "soldiers of the Virgin."*

## FIESTA DANCERS

The only remaining rituals of native origin are the performances of the *Pahkolas*, the *Maaso* or Deer Dancer, and the Coyote Society. Though the Pahkolas may appear at fiestas in their capacity as the hosts or "old men of the fiesta," they are best known and most often seen in connection with the Yaqui Deer Dance ceremony held at Easter. The Deer Dance itself is an ancient hunting ceremonial that dramatizes this once-important activity. Although these impersonators take part in the church processions, most of the dancing takes place in a small ramada at some distance from the chapel.

*The* Pahkolas *are generally thought of as the Old Men or hosts of the fiestas. During the Deer Dance they take the role of hunters. They may also take part in church processions.*

A chorus of three Deer Singers, who also play a water drum (a half gourd turned hollow side down in a bowl of water) and rasps, sing ancient hunting chants that poetically describe the world of the deer. A fourth musician simultaneously plays a two-piece bamboo flute and a flat, hide-covered drum.

The Pahkolas are aligned with the church when it is under attack by the Fariseos. During their own dances they act the part of clowns and entertain the spectators with jokes, pantomime, and horseplay.

The Pahkolas' dance has a shuffling step that emphasizes the soft rustling sound of their cocoon leg rattles. A jangling beat is provided by a wood rattle with metal disks, which is struck in the palm of one hand. When performing they wear a small wooden mask over the face—otherwise it is worn at the side of the head.

The Deer impersonator, the Maaso, wears a deer head when dancing. Red ribbons representing flowers are wound about the horns. The original purpose of this dance was to honor the deer so that it would allow itself to be caught by the hunters. The dance itself is a perfect pantomime of the deer's movements. More rapid and tense than the Pahkolas' dance, the Maaso maintains a steady "roll" with his gourd rattles, pausing occasionally to posture in imitation of a living deer.

## THE COYOTE DANCERS

The *Go'i* or Coyote Society is a military society responsible for the defense of the village and discipline within the village. The Coyote Dancers may appear at any Yaqui fiesta or *wardia*, where they set their chairs, perform their dances, and honor their saint.

They dance to songs composed about various animals, and carry bows on which they tap a beat with a bamboo staff. The drummer uses a flat hide-covered drum that is slightly smaller and higher in tone than that used by the drummer who accompanies the Maaso.

*The* Maaso *or Deer Dancer is an important and powerful figure to the Yaqui. Though he appears during the Yaqui Easter ceremonies—a basically Catholic event—he has ties to the ancient beliefs and religion of the Yaqui as they existed before the coming of the Europeans. Ryan Huna Smith*

# Peyote

Peyote (*Lophophora williamsii*) is a small turnip-shaped, spineless cactus that grows in the lower Rio Grande Valley from southern New Mexico and Texas southward to Nayarit, Mexico. It contains alkaloid substances that are hallucinogenic in nature—that is, they induce dreams or visions. Reactions to peyote seem to vary with the social situation under which it is used. In some it may merely cause nausea, while believers may experience optic, olfactory, and auditory sensations. They often report color visions, and say that the peyote may be "heard" singing or speaking. The effects wear off within 24 hours and leave no ill aftereffects. Peyote is non-addictive.

The use of peyote in rituals began in pre-Columbian times in Mexico. The Spaniards recorded its use by the Aztecs. It is still used today by the Tarahumara, Huichol, and Cora. Its purpose varies considerably, from use as a charm in footraces and hunting to a medicine in curing rites. It may also be employed to predict the weather or to locate lost objects (revelations appear in peyote-induced visions). Peyote also appears in elaborate rain-making ceremonies.

Peyote was introduced into the southern Plains in the 1840s. The Lipan Apache, Comanche, and Kiowa were the first tribes to adopt it. The first usage was primarily medicinal in nature—in the vision induced by peyote the patient made contact with supernatural powers that restored his health. Vomiting caused by nausea was believed to rid the body of the illness and spiritually purify it.

Occasionally peyote was used in connection with warfare—it revealed the location of the enemy by means of a vision or by speaking to the user.

From the southern Plains the use of peyote spread eastward to the Great Lakes regions and northward into parts of Canada. As it spread to other tribes, each group adapted peyote to fit their own cultural background. Following suppression of the Ghost Dance religion during the early reservation era, the peyote cult gained many followers. The drastic and demoralizing changes caused by reservation life made the Indian people receptive to a new religious philosophy that gave them a sense of well-being and pride, and stressed the importance of the "Indianness" of the participants. It was a religion of hope for a defeated people and its followers benefited spiritually, physically, and mentally.

It was at this time that the Native American Church had its beginnings. Drawing much from Christian teachings, it made use of peyote as a sacrament. The peyotists claim the white man had the Bible so he could learn about God—the Indian was given peyote for the same purpose. Biblical passages (all references to herbs are

K. C. DEN DOOVEN

*Shown here with a mescal bean necklace worn by some practitioners, are the peyote "buttons" which contain a hallucinogenic used to create the visions or dreams that are a part of the religious services of the Native American Church.*

*Peyote meetings may be held anywhere, but they are often held in tipis. In this drawing by a young Navajo child, the firelight inside the tipis silhouettes the participants. These services, which generally last all night, include singing (accompanied by drumming), prayers, contemplation, and communion with God, and end with a blessing. Consumption of peyote is not required. Darren Etcitty*

construed to include peyote) were often quoted to justify its use.

The Native American Church stresses a high moral code, which includes brotherly love, care of the family, self-reliance, and the avoidance of alcohol.

Incorporated in 1918, the N.A.C., whose membership is restricted to American Indians, is estimated to have 500,000 followers. Not all peyote users, however, are members of the church.

There has been much opposition to the peyote cults. Tribal members who follow their traditional religion are naturally upset over the introduction of a new religion, and oppose it on the grounds

that it is "foreign." Many Christian sects working among Indians oppose peyote because it "misinterprets" Christian beliefs to accommodate the use of peyote. Despite this opposition—and often because of it—the peyote cults continue to grow.

Tribes, states, and the federal government have had differing, evolving, and generally con-

The peyote box of a Road Chief includes rattles, fans, and a two-part staff, designed to fit in the box. They are frequently heavily beaded. A buckskin-covered metal drum, wooden beater, and eagle-bone whistle are also part of his belongings. The fan is used in blessing and purifying rites.

flicting legislation regarding the use of peyote. In 1994, federal legislation was finally passed that allows for the sacramental use of peyote by American Indians.

## NAVAJO PEYOTISM

Despite its early appearance in the Southwest, the use of peyote among Navajos was unknown until the 1920s. Southern Ute medicine men who used peyote to treat Navajo patients were the first contacts they had with either the cactus or the cult. The success of peyote as a medicine in the treatment of their illnesses led many of them to follow the "Peyote Road." Through the closely knit extended family and clan system, knowledge of peyotism spread.

Then, as now, many cult members continued to make use of traditional Navajo curing rites and, as with other tribal groups, modified the rituals to fit their own cultural traditions.

The rapid spread of peyotism on the Navajo reservation in the late 1930s is attributed to the economic stresses caused by the government's stock reduction program. As their way of life appeared to be threatened, some Navajos found a sense of security in the peyote religion.

The sudden increase in peyote users alarmed many traditionalists, government officials, and missionaries, and resulted in official action by the Navajo tribal council. In 1940 the sale, use, or possession of peyote on the Navajo reservation was declared an offense punishable by fine and/or imprisonment. Despite this prohibition the cult continued to grow. By 1950 an estimated 9,000 to 10,000 Navajos were peyotists. In 1965 the

number had grown to between 25,000 and 35,000 and is still increasing, with current estimates ranging up to 80,000. In 1967, the Navajo tribal council voted to allow use of peyote by N.A.C. members.

## PEYOTE CEREMONY

There is no strict service that must be followed in conducting peyote ceremonies either by members of the Native American Church or non-affiliated users.

Among the Navajo peyote users, ceremonies may be given to bless a new house, celebrate a birthday or special holiday, solemnize a wedding, ensure good health, cure an illness, or treat substance abuse problems.

The meeting is usually sponsored by a family who arranges for a Road Chief to conduct the ceremony and provides food and peyote buttons for guests.

The meeting, usually held in a hogan, though occasionally in a tipi, begins at sundown with preparation of a crescent-shaped altar by the Road Chief, and kindling of a ritually laid fire by the Fire Chief. The altar represents the universe to some, and the moon to others. A line drawn through the length of the crescent is symbolic of the Peyote Road. In the middle of the altar, on a bed of sage, is placed Chief (or Father) Peyote, a button of unusual size.

Other opening rites include the blessing and purifying—in cedar smoke—of the peyote paraphernalia. Sage is also smudged and passed around to be rubbed on the hands and body as a medicine.

Cigarettes are ritually smoked by all present,

four puffs each to the Road Chief, Mother Earth, and the participant as a blessing and prayer. Peyote buttons are then passed around for the members to eat.

The Road Chief begins the singing with four opening songs, followed by solo performances by the drummer and Cedar Chief and later by other members.

During the evening the fire is constantly tended by the Fire Chief whose duty it is to keep the fire and altar in order. During the course of the night he adds a "tail" of ash to the crescent altar, transforming it into an eagle or thunderbird.

At midnight the Road Chief sings another set of songs, and water is brought in to be drunk. More cigarettes are smoked as prayers, started by members and finished by the Road Chief, to assure that the prayers will be heard. The Road Chief then goes outside to blow an eagle bone whistle to call the spirits. Occasionally confessions or testimonials to the power of peyote may be given by those present.

If the ceremony is being conducted as a curing rite, the Road Chief chews a peyote button and gives it to the patient to swallow. He also purifies

him by fanning him with cedar smoke.

At first morning light water is again served by the Water Woman (sometimes called Peyote Woman), and the Road Chief sings his special morning water songs.

After the closing ceremony, which includes four more songs by the Road Chief, the ritual disposal of cigarette stubs, and final prayers, the people gather outdoors for a feast.

During the course of the evening an average of four buttons is consumed by each person present and participating. The successful worshipper may see visions, or hear peyote talk to him and instruct him on how to solve his problems or improve his life. If he is sick or depressed peyote may cure him. The evening is spent in contemplation and communion with God, with peyote serving as the sacrament. Occasionally cult members will eat a bit of peyote at other times as a prayer, but generally the belief is that peyote is not effective outside of meetings. The companionship of fellow peyote members also enhances the sense of well-being resulting from the use of peyote itself.

# Calendar of Southwestern Indian Ceremonials

Dates given here are approximate—ceremonies may be scheduled to fall on the nearest weekend to permit participation by tribal members who live or work in town. Many dances are scheduled a few weeks in advance or are announced annually.

Inquire locally for exact date and village if not given here. Also, due to the large numbers of visitors and periodic outrageous violations by non-Indians of tribal prohibitions against recording religious observances, not all of these ceremonials are still open to the public, and those that are may not be open every year.

NOTE: Taping, photographing, sketching, or note-taking at Indian ceremonials is generally strictly forbidden. In some cases photography anywhere on the reservation may be subject to paying a fee and receiving written permission. Even where photographs are being allowed, it is best to inquire first and receive formal permission. Please do not create unpleasant incidents by ignoring tribal regulations. For general conduct, a good rule of thumb is simply this: anything you would not hesitate to do (or wear) in your place of worship or community is probably also permissible at an Indian ceremonial or reservation.

## ARIZONA

| Date | Event | Tribe and Location |
|---|---|---|
| Feb.—usually last three weekends | Powamuy (Bean Dance). | Hopi—all villages. |
| February through April | Night Katsina Dances. | Hopi—all villages. |
| Easter—from Ash Wednesday through Easter | Easter Ceremonies. | Yaqui. Villages of Pascua, New Pascua, and Barrio Libre (Tucson) and Guadalupe (Tempe). |
| April through July | Daytime Katsina Dances. | Hopi—all villages. |
| June 24 | San Juan's Day—Chicken Pull. | Tohono O'odham, Santa Rosa, and other villages. |
| Late June or early July | Saguaro Wine Festival. | Tohono O'odham. Various villages. |
| Middle to late July | Niman (Home Dance). | Hopi—all villages. |
| July 30-31 | San Ignacio's Day. Fiesta and dances. | Yaqui—Pascua. |
| Middle to late August | Flute Dance. | Hopi. Odd years at Shipaulovi, Shungopavy, and Hotevilla. Even years at Mishongnovi and Walpi. |
| August, third weekend | Peach Festival. | Havasupai at Supai village. |
| October 4 and prior week | Fiesta of Saint Francis. | Yaqui and Tohono O'odham pilgrimage to Magdalena, Sonora. |

## NEW MEXICO

| Date | Event | Tribe and Location |
|---|---|---|
| January 1 | Tablita and Turtle Dances. | Cochiti, San Juan, Taos, and Zia. |
| January 6 | King's Day. Animal or Eagle dances in most Rio Grande pueblos. | Cochiti, Jemez, Sandia, San Juan, San Ildefonso, Tesuque, Taos, and Zia. |
| January 23 | Buffalo and Comanche Dances | San Ildefonso. |
| February—entire month | Frequent dances in most Rio Grande pueblos. | Inquire locally for time and place. |
| February 2 | Buffalo Dance. | San Felipe. |
| February 15 | Buffalo Dance. | San Juan. |
| March 19 | Fiesta and dances. | Laguna. |
| April 1 | Spring Corn or Tablita Dances. | Most pueblos. |
| Easter | Tablita Dances. Races. | Most pueblos. |
| May 1 | Tablita Dance. | San Felipe. |
| May 3 | Santa Cruz Day. Tablita Dance. | Taos. |
| May 3 | Tablita Dance and Coming of the River Men. | Cochiti. |
| June—first Saturday | Corn Dance. | Tesuque. |
| June | Katsina Dances. | Zuni. |
| June 8 | Buffalo Dance. | Santa Clara. |
| June 13 | San Antonio's Day. Tablita or Buffalo Dances. | Cochiti, Sandia, San Juan, Santa Clara, San Ildefonso, Taos, and Ysleta del Sur. |
| June 24 | San Juan's Day. Dances, races, and Chicken Pulls. | Acoma, Cochiti, Santa Ana, Santo Domingo, and Isleta. |
| July 4 | Nambe Ceremonial. | Nambe Falls. |

| Date | Event | Location |
|---|---|---|
| 4 | Mescalero Apache Gaan Dancers and Rodeo. | Mescalero. |
| 14 | San Buenaventura's Day. Tablita Dance. | Cochiti. |
| 25 and 26 | Santiago's and Santa Ana's Day. Corn Dances and Rabbit Hunt. | Acoma, Cochiti, Laguna, Santa Ana, and Taos. |
| July | Santa Clara Ceremonial at Puye´ Cliff Dwellings. | Puye´. |
| ust 2 | Old Pecos Bull Dance. | Jemez. |
| ust 4 | Corn Dance. | Santo Domingo. |
| ust 10 | San Lorenzo's Day. Fiesta and Corn Dances. | Picuris, Acomita, and Laguna. |
| ust 12 | Santa Clara's Day Dances. | Santa Clara. |
| ust 15 | Corn Dance. | Zia. |
| ust 15 | Harvest Dance. | Laguna (Mesita). |
| ust 28 | Fiesta. | Isleta. |
| tember 2 | Harvest Dance and Fiesta. | Acoma. |
| tember 4 | San Augustin's Day. Harvest Dance. | Isleta. |
| tember 8 | Harvest Dance. | Laguna (Encinal Village). |
| tember 8 | Corn Dance. | San Ildefonso. |
| tember 19 | Harvest Dance. | Laguna. |
| tember 25 | St. Elizabeth's Day. Corn Dances. | Laguna. |
| tember 29 | Various dances. | Taos. |
| tember 30 | San Geronimo's Day. Pole climbing by Koshares. Races, dances. | Taos. |
| tember—last week | Evergreen Dances. | Isleta (date announced annually). |
| | Harvest Dances. | San Juan (date announced annually). |
| ober 4 | Elk Dance and Fiesta. | Nambe. |
| ober 17 | Corn Dance. | Laguna (Paraje Village). |
| ember 12 | Corn Dance and Fiesta. | Jemez. |
| ember 12 | San Diego's Day. Animal Dances. | Tesuque. |
| November or early December | Shalako. | Zuni. |
| ember 12 | Matachine Dance. | Jemez. |
| ember 24 | Ceremonial dances in mission churches. Processions. | Most pueblos. |
| ember 25 | Various dances. | Most pueblos. |
| ember 26 | Turtle Dance. | San Juan. |
| ember 26 | Matachine Dance. | Taos. |
| ember 31 | Deer Dance. | Sandia. |
| December | Animal and other dances. | Most pueblos. |

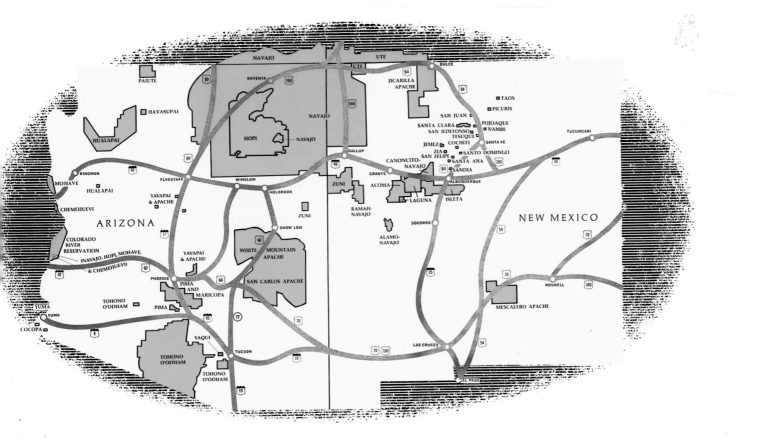

*The artwork of young children reflects the values and traditions of their culture. Santa Clara Pueblo artist, Heather Dashono, age 12, titled this work "Symbols of My Culture."*

## SUGGESTED READING

DOCKSTADER, FREDERICK J. *The Kachina and the White Man.* Albuquerque: University of New Mexico Press, 1985.

GONZALES, CLARA. *The Shalakos Are Coming.* Santa Fe: Museum of New Mexico Press, 1969.

GOODWIN, GRENVILLE. *Myths and Tales of the White Mountain Apache.* Tucson: University of Arizona Press, 1994.

GREEN, JESSE, ed. *Zuni: Selected Writings of Frank Hamilton Cushing.* Lincoln: University of Nebraska Press, 1979.

LABARRE, WESTON. *The Peyote Cult.* Hamden, Connecticut: Shoe String Press, 1959.

MATTHEWS, WASHINGTON. *Navaho Legends.* Salt Lake City: University of Utah Press, 1994.

MOON, SHEILA. *A Magic Dwells.* Middletown, Conn.: Wesleyan University Press, 1974.

ORTIZ, ALFONSO. *The Tewa World—Time, Being and Becom* *in a Pueblo Society.* Chicago, Illinois: University Chicago Press, 1969.

PAINTER, MURIEL T. *With Good Heart.* Tucson: University Arizona Press, 1986.

PARSONS, ELSIE C. *Pueblo Indian Religion.* (2 vols.) Linc University of Nebraska, 1996.

REICHARD, GLADYS A. *Navajo Religion.* Tucson: University Arizona Press, 1983.

SECAKUKU, ALPH. *Following the Sun and Moon.* Phoer Arizona: Heard Museum, 1995.

UNDERHILL, RUTH M. *Singing for Power—The Song Magi the Papago Indians of Southern Arizona.* Tucs University of Arizona Press, 1993.

*The Publisher gratefully acknowledges the use of original paintings from the following galleries and museums: Amerind Foundation, Inc.; James T. Bialac Collection; Elvis Torres Gallery; Simons Collection; and Oliver Enjady's private collection. Items photographed in this Southwestern Indian Trilogy came from numerous shops, museums, private collections, and individual Indian artisans. The work represents the broad range of items available for sale at reputable Indian arts and crafts shops nationwide.*

**Books on Indian Culture and the Southwest:** Southwestern Indian Arts and Crafts, Southwestern Indian Tribes, Southwestern Indian Ceremonials, Southwestern Indian Pottery, Southwestern Indian Weaving, Canyon de Chelly, Monument Valley, Mesa Verde, Grand Circle Adventure, The Rocks Begin to Speak, The Southern Paiutes, The Navajo Treaty, Zuni Fetishes. A hardbound edition combining the first 3 Southwestern Indian books is also available.

**Other Series by KC Publications:**

**Calendars** – For National Parks in dramatic full color, and a companion Color Your Own series, with crayons.

**The Story Behind the Scenery** - on America's national parks.

**in pictures** - companion series on America's national parks.

• **Translation Packages available.**

**Voyage of Discovery** - on the expansion of the western United States.

To receive our full-color catalog featuring over 135 titles—Books, Calendars, Screen Scenes, Videos, Audio Tapes, and other related specialty products:

**Call (800-626-9673), fax (702-433-3420), write to the address below,**
    **Or visit our web site at www.kcpublications.com**

**Published by KC Publications, 3245 E. Patrick Ln., Suite A, Las Vegas, NV 89120.**

*Inside back cover: Water serp rising in front of a Koshare, Rafael Medina, James T. Bialac Collect*

*Back cover: Rio Grande Pue Green Corn Dance, by J. D. Royl*

***Created, Designed, and Published in the U.***
Printed by Tien Wah Press (Pte.) Ltd, Singar
Pre-Press by United Graphic Pte.